A River
to Live By

A River to Live By

THE 12 LIFE PRINCIPLES OF MORITA THERAPY

DR. BRIAN OGAWA

Published by Xlibris/Random House

Library of Congress Control Number: 2007902170
ISBN: Hardcover   978-1-4257-8397-6
                    Softcover   978-1-4257-8393-8

To order additional copies of this book, contact:
Xlibris Corporation
1-888-795-4274
www.Xlibris.com
Orders@Xlibris.com
36451

CONTENTS

Dedicated to Brent Kalani, M.D. and Brooke Noelani, M.Ed. and those who give me the encouragement to write on matters dear to my soul and purpose.

Prologue

Shoma Morita, MD (1874-1938) was an eminent Japanese psychiatrist and university professor, who originated a prodigious therapy distilled from his medical training, clinical practice, and personal adversity. Morita therapy has proven effectual across cultures, and is now practiced and taught internationally. Although it was originally applied specifically to neurotic disorders such as anxiety, phobias, obsessive-compulsive behaviors, and psychosomatic illnesses, Morita therapy is presently administered in the treatment of a variety of psychological conditions, including depression, schizophrenia, borderline personality, bulimia nervosa, terminal illness, chronic pain, alcohol and drug addictions, and post trauma (Kitanishi & Mori, 1995; Ogawa, 1997, 1998, 1999).

There is no mystique to Morita therapy (LeVine, 1993). It offers conclusive intervention and counseling across the humanscape of stressful events. Morita was not only a pioneer of psychiatric theory but also a compassionate educator of successful everyday living. His focus was not strictly a medical construct of psychopathology and narrow symptomatic changes achieved through psychotherapy (Ishiyama, 1987). Morita modeled a *holistic* approach: the health of the whole person in every life circumstance. He summarized that optimal health results when the body, mind, and emotions are in their "natural flow." We live with the greatest energy and resilience when we do not obstruct this free and dependable course. The grace and power of a river thus became Morita's principal life metaphor.

The river has long been a popular imagery for a thriving life (Herendeen, 1986). Eastern philosophy and medicine, by and large, regard the "loss" or "blockage" of the flow of one's vital essence to be the cause of illnesses within oneself and disturbances in interpersonal relationships. Chinese Taoism, for example, deems the "best person" to be like water, soft and yielding, benefiting all and not competing (Lao-Tzu, 604-531 BC). In the West, William James likened a healthy mind to a "stream of consciousness": our psychic life has "flights and perchings," a series of transitions and resting places (James, 1890). As Palmer (2006) further muses:

> In seeing the whole river from beginning to end, I found that it offered values . . . [The] source and headwaters symbolize youth. The small but increasing flow offers promises of many kinds. Growing larger, the river reflects adolescence, and the rapids are chaotic, risky, exciting. Then the widening waters signify maturity. Some rapids here are huge, and in other places headwinds blow upriver through miles of flatwater. Finally, with a broad and gentle current the lower river denotes old age, the mysterious and infinite ocean ahead.
>
> (p. 29)

I have, consonantly, portrayed the twelve life principles of Morita therapy as parallel and complementary river currents. The harmony of these currents generates the momentum for us to live strong and sound. In Japanese culture, the suffix — dō characterizes a verifiable lifeway. Morita-dō can assuredly guide anyone on life's journey. Its principles proliferate teachings from traditional Japanese culture and Eastern philosophy, but also strike a responsive transcultural, universal, and timeless chord.

Acknowledgments

My first instruction in Morita life principles and Eastern lifeways was unknowingly through my parents. My father, Masanobu Ogawa, emigrated from Shikoku Island in southern Japan to Seattle, Washington at the age of 17. My mother, Tsutako Tanaka, was born in Montebello, California to flower growers, who had earlier worked as immigrant contract laborers in the sugar plantation fields of Waialua, Hawaii in the late 1890's. My parents predictably raised me according to the values of their Japanese heritage, including Buddhism and Shinto.

Throughout my professional and academic career, my parental tutelage was revisited and clarified through my mentors in Morita therapy. I am most indebted to the following: Dr. Michio Kusama of San Francisco, who copiously shared with me his translations of Morita's voluminous works and was a thoughtful friend; The Rev. Iwao Tanishima, whose Morita therapy group I studied with for two years; the late Mr. Yozo Hasegawa, Mr. Hiroshi Yokoyama, Ms. Mikako Ito, and Ms. Junko Fujimoto of Seikatsu No Hakkenkai; the late Dr. Takehisa Kora (Dr. Morita's primary successor); Dr. Kenji Kitanishi of Japan Women's University; Dr. Kei Nakamura and Dr. Mikiko Kubota of Jikei Medical University; Dr. and Mrs. Chihiro Fujita of Tokiwadai-Shinkeikai; Dr. Chika Higa, Dr. Noriaki Harada, and Mr. Minami of Higa Mental Health Clinic; Dr. Ishu Ishiyama of the University of British Columbia, who has played a key role in forging the teaching of "Moritian" theory in the West; Dr. Noriaki Azuma of Iwate University, who conducts research on the application of Morita across cultures and disciplines, and who greatly assisted me in my most recent visits to Japan; Dr. Akihisa

Kondo, whose translations of Dr. Morita are invaluable; Dr. Peg LeVine of the University of Tasmania for her warmth and brilliance; Dr. Natalia Semenova, who directs the Morita Information Center in Russia; and Drs. Zucheng Wang, Haiyin Zhang, and Zeping Zhao, who organized the Fifth International Meeting for Morita Therapy in Shanghai, China.

To the supportive peers who have integrated Morita principles into their lives and professions, I am grateful for your lasting friendships: Gretchen Howard, Helen Marie Thueson-Stone, Karen M. Parker, Sharon Stewart, Helen P. Smith-Bradley, Betsy Pape, Dr. Mary Samuel Reid, Theresa Benson, Karen Kalergis, and Amy Wong Mok.

To the Washburn University students who patiently consider my views, I thank you for your openness. These include those who are the very first to receive advanced Morita studies: Toni Wash, Caroline Grantham, Devan Tucking, Krystal Boxum-Debolt, Lawrence Bridgforth, James Hurt, Martha Venzor, Susan Bernstein, Lori Huske, Jodell Langley, Nancy Way, Melissa McCoy, Denise Cook, Carol Prim, Frances Boudreau, Rebeca Garcia, and Lori Winchell. Finally, to my colleagues at Washburn University, I am indebted for providing me with the setting for scholarship and collegiality during these past years: Baili Zhang of International Programs; Dr. Willie Dunlap and Dr. Dan Petersen of the School of Applied Studies; Dr. Rick Ellis, Dr. Deborah Altus, Dr. Diane McMillen, Dr. Iris Wilkinson, Dr. Jo Ramburg, Dave Skinner, Nancy Breske, Jacque Ford, and Dr. Malcolm Smith of the Department of Human Services; and Dr. Ron Wasserstein, Vice President of Academic Affairs.

Introduction

Mizu

Japan is a thickly mountainous nation with ranges forming a long spine bisecting the cardinal islands in the archipelago. Japan's numerous rivers (*kawa*) are, consequently, relatively short with steep channel slopes. The longest river is the Shinano-gawa (228 miles), which arises from Mount Kobushi in the Japanese Alps of Honshu and empties into the Sea of Japan. The country also has nearly double the world's average of precipitation, mostly occurring during the *tsuyu* ("rainy season") and monsoon period. These topographic and climatic conditions produce rapid-flowing rivers that crosscut through the mountains and are prone to flooding. The peak flow discharge to basins ranges from 10 to 100 times the major rivers of other countries. The regime coefficient (ratio of maximum to minimum discharge) is between 200 and 400 times larger than that of continental rivers (River Bureau, 2006).

Since early times the Japanese have made abundant use of the alluvial plains and lowlands created by large sediment runoff. Many of Japan's prominent communities have developed along rivers, including those devoted to the farming of staple rice crops. The rivers thus have represented the central themes of Japanese life: blessing and danger, sustenance and disaster. Their precipitous run to the sea and perpetual overflow has also meant that Japan's plenteous rivers—the nations' most important water resource—ironically contribute to the recurring reality of shortages. The high population density of Japan requires the most efficient conservation and prudent use of natural river water. The vast watershed of the Tone-gawa, for example, must sate the more than 30 million inhabitants of the Tokyo metropolitan area.

Whole civilizations have soared or collapsed with the sufficiency or scarcity of pure water (*mizu*). All life, categorically, would powderize and vanish without ample, aseptic water. Water defines a living being from a dead thing. As Callahan (1998) writes, we are not earth creatures who occasionally require a little water; we are water creatures. Without water we are simply heaps of salt and carbon, phosphorous and sulfur-ash waiting to be scattered by the first dry breeze (p. 9). Water molecules are dynamic participants in every biochemical action for human energy generation, muscle contraction, tissue repair, body temperature regulation, and waste transport (Joiner-Bey, 2002, pp. 62-63). The human brain is comprised of 70% water, lungs nearly 90%, and blood 83%. Our internal rivers of water are the super arteries that scrupulously keep us from withering and perishing.

W.H. Auden (1907-1973) tersely wrote: "Thousands have lived without love; not one without water." Even though a mere .006% of the earth's freshwater is found in rivers, most of the water we use to sustain everyday life comes from this source (Gleick, 1996). Rivers are the water cache of the world (Palmer, 2006, p. 41). *Flowing water* (*mizu no nagare*), inasmuch, eloquently symbolizes the very survival and healthy course of human life.

Free-flowing

In his magnificent photographic essay, *Rivers of America*, Palmer (2006) laments the plight of the Ohio River recalled from his childhood. He refers to the river as the "largest barge-floating cesspool in America." The many rivulets that pour into it have inherited the *wrong* river. The Ohio, the largest river between the Mississippi and the Appalachian Mountains, has been abused by aging steel mills rusting along its edge, traffic pounding its banks, and railroad tracks cordoning off the water. The river is not a life birthing and sustaining ecosystem but a murderous conduit for toxic waste and sludge in obscene volumes and concentrations. The Ohio is a denatured behemoth and public health hazard. It is what a river should *not* be: it is plodding and belligerent, and it stinks (p. 24).

Palmer recognizes that even dirty water reeking of desperation can be cleaned up — a gargantuan undertaking in the case of the Ohio River. The Ohio in preindustrial America was the biologically richest in our nation; it was big and unspoiled. Virgin waters, however, play mostly in our imagination. There are very few unfettered rivers anywhere. What troubles Palmer most is the primary reason for the Ohio's demise and menace: it has no flow. It doesn't *move*. The Ohio is dammed back-to-back twenty-six times in 981 miles — scarcely a hundred yards of free-flowing current to be found in its entire length. In fact, less than 2% of our total mileage of rivers and streams in America flow in a completely natural condition. There are 75,000 sizeable dams that shunt and block river flow across the continent (Palmer, 2006, pp. 24, 184).

In contrast, the Shimanto-gawa, the longest river in Kochi Prefecture on Shikoku Island (the province of Morita's birth and childhood as well as that of my father) has a rare intimate relationship with local riverbank residents. The Shimanto-gawa has 300 tributaries and runs 122 miles from Mt. Irazu to the Pacific Ocean at Tosa Bay. It is revered as the last unspoiled, *free-flowing* river in Japan. It is the only major river that is not artificially dammed anywhere along its course to the sea (Japan Atlas, 2006). The Shimanto-gawa is also Japan's *cleanest* river — it has escaped being poisoned and ruined — due to minimal industrialization along its banks and the green diligence of Shikoku residents. Its biologically splendid water has 94 species of wild fish — the most of all rivers of Japan. The Shimanto-gawa's crystal-clarity, moreover, invites residents to flock to it — rather than flee from it — for their livelihood, recreation, and religious purification ceremonies. The river is not something to contend with and subdue. Honored in its pristine nature, it offers a resource for the residents to better their lives. The veneration accorded to the peaceful and unhindered Shimanto-gawa may well have been part of the inspiration for Morita's river metaphor for wellbeing.

Waterway

In the discipline of Zen, the aim is to yield a person who is *unsui* ("cloud-water"): one who drifts like clouds and flows like water (Kapleau, 1989). The Zenist, through a meditative and minimalist life and practice of the "waterway," seeks to attain freedom, spontaneity, and pliability to adjust to changing circumstances without destructive consequences. The Morita paradigm for living also extols the *staying power* of rivers throughout moments of flux and fury. Rivers, on their journey, assume many forms: lean and fast to expansive and dawdling. Our lives equally churn with every mood and pace: unbridled like a raging torrent and whispering like a velvety brook.

Rivers invariably do encounter a succession of obstructions as they wend their way from headwaters to end: immoveable hills, fallen trees, protruding boulders, and assorted rubble. Rivers, however, do not dissipate because of these seemingly infinite obstacles. They maneuver through, curl around, surge over, and seep beneath to maintain their progression. This bold authority of water is archetypically seen in the longest of the world's rivers, the perennial Nile. Descending 4,160 miles south to north, unaided by tributaries, the Nile forms our very concept of a river (Herendeen, 1986, p. 25). Its veritable reliability projects promise and peril: fertile valleys bounded by uncultivable deserts, beneficial irrigation and unfavorable floods. Like all great rivers, the Nile is "holy water." As Herendeen (1986) writes, these rivers not only support life but make attainable a life of plenty. Posed precariously on their banks is a wary *and* grateful humanity (p. 24).

Even when rivers subside into seasonal trickles or obscure in the blackout of highway culverts, they wondrously reappear. In the aftermath of fierce cascades and falls, rivers also rebound and resume — their spray and mist settling into renewed (and altered) flow. Weary at times from all the flashing bends and rock-ribbed rapids (cf. Palmer, 2006), rivers may seek out respite in wayside pools and shadowy eddies. If they detour here too long, they decline into a languorous bog. A new rush and flush of current — at the onset of spring or emboldened by raindrops and snowflakes received into watersheds and tributaries — thrusts the rivers forward with liberating momentum. Rivers persist in their episodic passage toward receptive lakes (*mizuumi*) and welcoming seas (*umi*).

In the same manner, our lives are engaged with a jagged sequence of heartaches, predicaments, and hazards — cross currents to living well. Crises (*kiki*) are like non-negotiable waterfalls: our sense of happiness and security plummets in shock and confusion.

Contrastingly, long-suffering is like a listless whirlpool going downward and nowhere, threatening to frustrate our dreams and hopes. At times, we even become our own barriers to living well, mired in self-doubt and self-recrimination. Through the breadth of these life events, we can persevere. We do not always set the conditions or control the situations in which we find ourselves, but we always assume accountability for how we respond. Our mettle may be severely tested, but we are not deterred because of the unfailing and purposeful movement of life.

Chapter 1

Morita Life Principle One Attention

"Life flows from being observant"

*Healthy attention is a fluid state
without attachment, fully alert to
the whole environment.*

Shoma Morita
(1928/1974, p. 99)

Rhythm of attention

Life *is* attention (*chūmoku*). It is the journaling of each person, place, subject, idea, and emotion that has nudged our notice, entertained our interest, or sustained our concentration. The care and consideration by which we confer our attention, therefore, ultimately defines, characterizes, and mirrors who we are. *We are what we attend to!*

One day a man of the people said to Zen Master

Ikkyu: "Master, will you please write for me some maxims of the highest wisdom?"

Ikkyu immediately took his brush and wrote the word, "Attention."

"Is that all?" asked the man. "Will you not add anything more?"

Ikkyu then wrote twice running, "Attention. Attention."

"Well," remarked the man rather irritably, "I really do not see much depth or subtlety in what you have just written."

Then Ikkyu wrote the same word three times running: "Attention. Attention. Attention."

Half-angered, the man demanded: "What does that word Attention mean anyway?"
And Ikkyu answered gently: "Attention means attention."
(Kapleau, 1967, pp. 10-11)

Consider the quintessential human endeavor of "love" (*ai*). Each one of us is capable of loving because the principal work that loves takes is attention (cf. Peck, 2002). *Unconditional love is unconditional attention.* When we love someone, we commit to giving our fullest attention to that person's welfare, needs, and concerns. The opposite of love is apathy or indifference. To be ignored, overlooked, or forgotten is the antithesis of being in a loving relationship. To live gloriously or love splendidly means to attend well. Our lives are enriched and love burgeons the more we pay attention.

When we attend to what is most "significant" in a given moment, our lives flow to a natural rhythm. Morita (Kondo in Morita, 1928/1998, p. xix) termed this *mushoju-shin* ("widening of awakeness") and *akiraka ni miwakeru-koto* ("clear discernment"). A soaring eagle, for example, has the virtues of both an expansive view of its domain and the gaze to pinpoint its quarry. We also score our "marks" in life when our unique responses come from a healthy awareness of our circumstances. Those, however, who have either an excessive *or* insufficient responsiveness often suffer from physical and mental distress. These persons adapt poorly to situations and relate to the external world with either extreme sensitivity or blanket dullness (Morita, 1928/1998, p. 132).

Just as music streams into a symphony, our attention flows into our life song. Conversely, just as a wayward sour note ruins a melody, misappropriation of attention obstructs our focus on what is most immediate and, accordingly, most vital. Concerts are not composed from an isochronous lone verse, and our lives are not fulfilled by facsimile events. Limitless subjects and eclectic attention dramatically lyricize our lives.

Wabi-sabi

Novelist Nicholson Baker (2003) writes frequently about the minutiae of daily life. Baker lives with little pretense. He awakens each morning at 4:45, strikes a match to light the stove, and sits down with his mug of coffee. His "insightful moments" ramble from observing his pet duck pecking his cat's behind to witnessing the sudden howl of light when he cracks open his refrigerator in the dark. Are these moments too inconsequential to revel in, or do they bespeak the cadence of Baker's life?

Most of us would never be accused of overattending to such "negligible" events. We are more likely to *under*attend, routinely dismissing the pecking duck and howling light as not remotely contributing to anything about the real meaning of life. These occupy the faraway ditches, basements, and dumps for those things that matter little or lack aesthetics. For Baker, however, being "free" to love the day's happenstance is the ready means to find life's missing meaning. If "trivia" dominates everyday living, by slighting such do we trivialize life itself? If we can find passion in "minor matters," can we then perhaps find it in *many* things? Paying attention to these at least would keep us from living in a blur, whereby hours, days, and years pass by without attaching to anything. Life flows from attending to the "intricacy of living."

Wabi-sabi is the beloved Japanese term for the kind of beauty that is imperfect, transitory, and incomplete (Koren, 1994). This confounds the notion that beauty is reserved only for the monumental, spectacular, and enduring. It is about the infinitesimal and hidden, the tentative and ephemeral — things so slight and understated they are almost invisible at first glance. *Wabi* ("quiet" or "tranquil") and *sabi* (the "patina" that results from graceful aging) also connote refined simplicity, something without excess ornamentation or clutter (Lafayette De Mente, 1997, pp. 308, 383). *Wabi-sabi* is indeed elementary of anything "Japanese" — whether a decoration, tool, craft, accessory, scene, or garden. Japanese are said to know instantly if something has the *wabi* look, a below-the-surface appeal.

Philosophized as a lifeway *wabi-sabi* represents the "small wonders" and "secret joys" inconspicuous within everyday passing moments but ultimately telling of a full life. As a knowledgeable jeweler once shared with me, the Japanese prefer their time-worn wedding bands to be not too highly resurfaced or polished in the (misguided) attempt to remove scratches and restore original luster. The numerous nicks compellingly recall the defining experiences of marital life. The common Western preference for mint condition tends to deprive objects of their indelible history (Keene, 1989, p. 134).

It is sheer impossibility that we notice *everything*. The mind flows constantly in and out of awareness like the "wavering reflections of sunbeams on the rotating water of a watermill" (Morita, 1928/1998, p. 119). It is also dubious that everything has the same degree of urgency and import. A sleeping mother awakens when her sick child coughs, but does not at the roar of thunder. To what each of us gives our attention and appreciation (and their close relative, interest) is a "personal investment." As California psychiatrist and wellness author Dean Ornish (2000) prescribes, we enormously profit from just being attentive. Paying attention lets us enjoy life more. Whether it's food, sex, music, massage, art or anything else involving our senses, we'll enjoy it more when we are fully present and not distracted. Attention is energy and also reproduces energy when used. It is like the battery in a car that recharges itself in the running of the motor (Scaravelli, 1991). We steadily increase our "availability" for stimulation and inspiration.

Noiseless

Paulson (1999) laments that modernistic, techno-digital life has landed us in a maelstrom of information with too little time to find and digest wisdom. We are enfeebled with a short attention span, a constant need to be entertained or shocked, and an inability to look at anything in depth (p. 4). One of the ways to rectify this inattentiveness is to engage in protracted periods of silence, because meddling clatter and clamor make us less mindful and perceptive. We are prone to be more resourceful in our actions when babel and bedlam are missing.

During Morita intensive workshops, I therefore assign an entire afternoon in which conversation is not permitted and noise of any kind must be kept to a minimum. Use of hand gestures, facial clues, and expressive mime come to the fore, resulting in the participants paying *more* attention in order to communicate. As they strive to be exceedingly quiet in every action, overall awareness also opens up. Subdued walking, for example, causes them to walk more softly and efficiently as well as to be more considerate, less damaging, progressively smooth, and "non-violent." This is similar to *kinhin* in which Zenists walk in simple, measured steps to enhance meditation and to train respect for each person and object in their path and lives (Ives, 1992). In quietude, in other words, there is less distortion of thoughts and minimization of the overt effects of our behaviors. *The more we are purposefully attentive, the more we see the purpose in being attentive.*

During the period of silence at a Gainesville, Florida workshop, the attendees were invited to find petrified sharks' teeth embedded for eons in the nearby streambed. We were astonished that these remnants of marine life could be found hundreds of miles from the present-day Atlantic and Gulf shorelines. The teeth came from a variety of sharks and thus were of vastly different dimensions and tints. The attendees needed alert eyes to determine a shark's tooth from a broken shell or chipped pebble in the mud. While searching for sharks' teeth, they were also instructed to collect litter strewn along the stream banks, floating in the water, or submerged in the sediment. Bent aluminum cans, shards of broken bottles, bits of plastics, shreds of papers, and miscellaneous trash were to be bagged and carried away. In their hunt for prized shark teeth, would they be conscientious about plain rubbish? Would they, moreover, be wonderfully awake to the reprieve of the cool water in the torrid mugginess, squish of creek clay between their toes, and wind rustling through the everglade trees? Would they be aware of both the human imprint on the environment *and* its largesse for them?

Adaptation and self-preservation

Morita (1928/1998) categorized how we attend in two ways: "unconscious attention" and "conscious attention." Unconscious attention is operating when we are involved in instinctive behaviors or habitual activities. These do not demand vigorous attention because we engage in these activities often. Once initiated, we seem to glide through these actions, not thoughtlessly, but without a second thought. Morita (1928/1998) compared this to the great care it takes at first to play music or make handicrafts. Once we become skilled, we are less aware of the details of the activity. As *any* action becomes less awkward and commonplace, we no longer scrutinate its finite aspects but concentrate more on its intended purpose. Attention then becomes "centrifugally-oriented" (p. 120).

The Japanese, for example, routinely eat with utilitarian *hashi* ("chopsticks") that have become like "bamboo appendages." The more skillfully one employs *hashi*, the more one can concentrate on the meal itself. When children or beginners are learning to manipulate *hashi*, they will likely be highly conscious (and self-conscious) about the oddity of plying two sticks to pick up a liberal assortment of food shapes and sizes. Another illustration of unconscious attention is when we become habituated to a certain sound. We may "hear" that sound but not inventory it because we are no longer attentively listening to it. The ticking clock, rotating ceiling fan, spinning computer hard drive, or humming traffic becomes barely and intermittently audible "white noise." This usually occurs when our attention is preoccupied by some immediate task.

Conscious attention occurs when the mind naturally attends to new stimuli or experiences that necessitate a heightened level of exertion to meet novel demands. Novelty is matter-of-fact for Moritists:

Hajimete no kodo ni fuan ha tukimono.

We always have anxiety when we do
new things for the first time.
                                  (Hasegawa, 1993, p. 6)

Such consciousness, Morita (1928/1998) wrote, is "like water that flows through a valley, breaks on the rocks, makes a deep pool, fills a river, and eventually enters the sea" (p. 120). We instinctively move with *adaptation* and *self-preservation* in mind, especially when a critical or life-or-death matter is before us. For example, we could walk the length of a gnarl-free plank lying on a level floor with comparative aplomb. A misstep would hardly be perilous. But what if we must walk on a moss-slippery log bridging 100 feet above a wild river studded with massive angular boulders? Under these circumstances, we should calibrate each move as we proceed. To be timidly clumsy or divided in our attention would be disastrous (Morita, 1928/1974, pp. 82-83)!

This amplification of attention is finely executed by elite mountain climbers. The ultimate challenge for avid climbers is arguably Mt. Everest, the crown of the world at 29,035 feet. Sherpa Tenzing Norgay and New Zealander Sir Edmund Hillary were the first to reach the top on May 29, 1953. Since then, Mt. Everest has been surmounted more than 1,000 times, although 180 climbers have also perished on its slopes. The aspiring climber of Mt. Everest must painstakingly control each repetitive segment of the long ascent: *this* crevice, *this* handhold, and *this* toe-plant. The slightest inattention can cost the climber's life. This sobering fear helps to prevent mistakes.

*De*scending Mt. Everest, however, is also extremely hazardous. Davo Karnicar, a Slovenian, *skied* down from the peak to a base camp at 17,515 feet! The harrowing tumble down the mountain took four hours and 40 minutes of sheer will, astounding skill, and unbridled luck. At one point, Karnicar stopped momentarily to rest, only to find that he was staring at two legs grotesquely sticking out of the snow. The legs belonged to one of the fatalities of a 1996 ice storm. Karnicar suddenly realized that he was on the climber's chest! Too late to rethink attempting the descent at all, and too early to hurrah at arriving alive at the finish, Karnicar became even more focused on skiing safely down the frozen river slopes. This was his only real option, because inattentiveness would leave him vulnerable. He knew that each skill must be matched with what was *being tested at that moment* (Tresniowski & Finan, 2000). Fortuitously, not everything is so precarious in life, but the caveat still holds: we lose our life as we lose our attention.

Color blue

We all have "selective attention" that relegates us to an abridged version of reality. This results from the way we filter our experiences and the sensory load we can process (Sheikh & Sheikh, 1989, p. 428). For example, recall what you noticed was the color blue (*aoi*) over the previous few hours: the sky, tableware, furnishings, apparel, edifices, and art. Your list might be extensive or paltry depending upon your "affinity" to blue. Another person, even a close companion throughout this day, may or may not have glimpsed the very same things. Certain elements of reality pique our attention while others do not interest us at all. That is why when pickpockets stand in a crowd of saints, all they see are their pockets (Hari Dass Baba in Millman, 1992, p. 42)!

If you were subsequently given the instruction to jot down, over the next several hours, everything you happened upon that was the color blue, what would occur? That lamina of reality — the color blue — would leap out from everywhere! Your notations would be much more wide-ranging because you are *deliberately* searching out the color blue. What was previously glossed over is now a vivid parade. In the same regard, if we target the evil and violence committed in our world, dismay and cynicism would ensue. There are inexhaustible ways humans mistreat one another. During my term as a Los Angeles deputy medical-examiner coroner in behavioral analysis, I witnessed how death is too often the result of some despicable viciousness or cruelty. Every manner of unnatural death is rained upon this city: decapitation, bludgeoning, strangulation, and impalement. "There are two dangers in this world: a dangerous river and a dangerous heart, but the latter is even more so" (Chinese proverb in Char, 1970, p. 27).

Overattention to the worst in humankind is bruising and wearisome, but when we do seek out the courteous, kind, and generous actions of others, grace is also rife. When we are overly guarded or suspicious, we underrate others. This does not mean to ladle cheer on blatant acts of heartlessness and injustice. Overrating has its own shams and pitfalls. Instead, we are to live *realistically* and *openly*. This occurs, according to Kora (1990, p. 11), when subjective experience (what we perceive to be) and objective knowledge (what is) *coincide*. If we are fluid in our attention, the ledger of life tallies both credits and debits.

Rush hour "madness"

Years ago, I was invited to conduct staff training at a state mental health hospital in California. On my drive onto the facility grounds that first morning, a person who appeared to be a patient was directing traffic at a three-way intersection without signal lights. The glaring patient raised his hand to motion me to stop, and I instantly complied. I then watched as he expertly routed the traffic flow during this peak rush hour. After some 20 seconds, I was waved forward. When my passenger, one of the hospital therapists, and I arrived at the staff parking lot, I paused and asked if that was indeed a patient directing traffic. "Yes," she answered. I inquired as to his diagnosis and prognosis. "Bill," she said, suffered from paranoid schizophrenia, had been at the hospital for about eight years, and would likely be institutionalized for a lengthy period. He was being treated, as most other patients at the hospital, with psychotropic medication, limited occupational therapy, and weekly group sessions. These were employed for patient management more than curative purposes.

Bill, I was also told, had been directing traffic every morning for several years, on his own initiative and without administrative authorization or interference. I asked the therapist how many collisions or mishaps had Bill caused during that period. The therapist, reflecting for a few moments, could not recall a single incident! Bill was visibly not "out of touch with reality," and in a sense was providing his own "therapy." He had constricted his life to what he deemed important (directing traffic), and, interestingly, was exceedingly helpful to others. Bill basically was not any different than anyone of us in being selectively attentive. In fact, in this specific pursuit at least, he was observably superior! How many of us would have been frazzled by the commotion of converging traffic? We might well have caused any number of fender-benders and snarls.

Bill, of course, could benefit from broadening and redirecting his attention beyond just this preoccupation. What had caused him to become so narrowly functional, and for the most part inattentive to other areas of his life, is unclear. Nuances of brain chemistry, childhood trauma, or severe relational troubles may all have contributed to some degree. The process of (extreme) attachment to certain areas of life and (virtual) exclusion of others, however, is not merely an "abnormal" trait of those we have labeled "mentally ill." Whatever we do (well) is very much connected to and made possible by the attention we bring to bear upon it.

Joriki

There must be a healthful balance between sharp focus and diffused awareness to allow our attention to readily shift whenever prudent or pressing within the context of the moment (Morita, 1928/1998, p. 104). In the state of full attention or acute concentration, the mind is actively directed toward the salient object in the surroundings, and therefore can smoothly make the shift. *Joriki* is this "one-pointedness" that allows us to "act instantly" in a manner wholly appropriate to circumstances (Yasutani-roshi in Kapleau, 1967).

In the state of fixation or absorption (*toraware*), however, the mind is passive and caught by the object of attention and is less free to switch (Frager, u.d., p. 51). For example, when reading this book, the tip of your nose is in your field of vision. Yet, as Morita (1928/1998) explains, you are not aware of your nose because "the eye is blind if the mind is absent" (p. 71). The development of an obsessive disorder depends on whether you ignore the nose or fixate on it. If you become mentally preoccupied with somehow removing your nose from your field of vision, you become blocked from reading. Acknowledging the nose, as it naturally exists, enables you to continue reading.

Fixation traps us in a static perception of what is "worthy" of our attention. If we overattach to a personal flaw or symptom of disease (or any internal or external object), we ignore the panorama of life (Morita, 1928/1998, p. 101). To prevent this foolhardy "unchanging focus in an ever-changing world," we must practice "peripheral attention." This does not mean a scattered mind but rather complete alertness and aliveness. A clear and active mind, in other words, finds harmony between mental introversion and extroversion. Introverts are very self-conscious and concerned with the details of their physical and mental discomforts. They are more likely to become dependent, depressed, or egocentric. In contrast, extroverts overattend to their social and physical environments and become careless, are frequently overextended, and spend little time nurturing their health. When either inclination predominates, psychological imbalance occurs (Morita, 1928/1998, pp. 106-107).

Fixation is *not* the same as concentration, the temporary exclusion of irrelevant stimuli and untimely matters in order to accomplish the task at hand. In concentration, the mind is calm and receptive, guiding us to truly benefit from the always evolving and sometimes complicated circumstances of our lives (cf. T. Nakamura in Frager, u.d., p. 52). As Karen Parker (1998), a Moritist yoga instructor, states, "When we are attentive and fully concentrated, there is a unique energy of doing—the coming together of body, mind, and soul" (p. 2).

Merging Currents: Attention is refined by intention.

Chapter 2

Morita Life Principle Two Intention

"Life flows from being purposeful"

Sandokai (one of the Zen classics) states, "If we walk without knowing the way, merely going forward will not yield the right path. Distance does not matter. What matters is the right path; going astray leads one far away from the right path."

Shoma Morita
(1928/1998, p. 78)

Ennui

Rivers do not always hasten to their denouement. Some rivers ambitionless zigzag the land. Cather (1997), for example, describes one peculiar turbid little stream in the Solomon Valley of western Kansas that "crawls along between naked bluffs, choked and split by sand bars" (p. 357). The Solomon is heartily disgusted with the country through which it flows, but it makes no haste to quit it. It is one of the "most futile little streams under the sun," and never gets anywhere. The Solomon's current is sluggish and buries itself in the mud until it literally dries up from weariness and ennui, without ever reaching anything. Hot winds buffet the valley and river. In time, the stream tires of giving its meager strength to moisten fields that remain barren and corn that never matures. Its watermarks are scarcely discernible.

Life to some people can seem scabrous and pointless. They are unable to nurture themselves or others. They are like the languid and apathetic Solomon: "chronically bewildered" and lacking a sense of orientation (cf. Banks, 1983, p. 104). Still others may frenetically chase splashes of interests. Their days are interspersed with loose specks of excitement. Life, regardless, is not how fast we live but what direction we take. An inch deviation at the outset culminates in a thousand miles off course (Morita, 1928/1998, p. 96). As the journalistic legend Edward R. Murrow, in the prologue to the 1956 film, *Around the World in 80 Days*, forewarned: "Speed is good, only when wisdom leads the way."

The anemic Solomon is nothing like the Mississippi, which carries one and a half times the water of the next largest river in North America, disgorging 593,000 cubic feet per second. Bubbling forth from subterranean springs in the remote corner of northwestern Minnesota, its odyssey traverses 2,500 miles to the Gulf of Mexico. It is by all accounts nature's fluid highway and flowing honey as it swells to enormous size and supports life and livelihood along its way (Kelman, 2003). A hundred thousand creeks, rivulets, and tributaries will join this nascent tiny brook to become a grand watercourse, potent landscaper, and major shipping channel. The Mississippi is the "ultimate accumulator": it drains an area reaching to 300 miles from the shore of the Atlantic and 500 miles from the Pacific coastline (Palmer, 2006, p. 69). The Mississippi *knows where it is going and how to get there.*

Kata

The Japanese have traditionally proscribed behavior by cultural rules and norms termed *kata.* This detailed system—tied to age, gender, birth order, social position, and employment status—facilitates prediction of exactly how persons in social situations will behave. *Kata* thus helps to offset disappointment and shame (Weisz,

Eastman, & McCarty, 1996, p. 67). The precise forms and protocol of *kata* are fitted for every aspect of shared life in the home, business, and community. The Japanese are "etiquette obsessed" and frown upon lame or inexact behavior. Tactfulness, discretion, and deference are noticed and valued while intrusiveness, witlessness, and ebullience are noted and admonished.

Some non-Japanese unfavorably caricature *kata* as robotic. They refer to the Japanese people as "acting like ants" or "moving like grains of sand." If you have ever ventured into the subway and rail hubs of Tokyo's metropolitan area, you might agree as you surveyed the blank looks on the faces of those hurrying to places of work, school, or shopping. Shinjuku Station, for example, is inundated with an astounding 2-3 million travelers per day. However, you would also endorse the upshot of *kata*: rarely do these commuters unceremoniously bump into or jostle one another. The Japanese coolly and reflexively slide through this human river while unsuspecting tourists can be swept away. The Japanese have an antennae sense of their body movements and personal actions because of the countless daily *kata* they tacitly perform.

Kata actually have their genesis in the copious religious rituals that were an integral part of Japanese life from the earliest times (Lafayette De Mente, 1997, p. 18). These rituals developed into models for a strict master-apprentice approach to teaching crafts and arts, including the martial arts such as judo and kendo, and aesthetic arts such as *shodō* ("calligraphy"), *sadō* ("tea ceremony"), and *kadō* ("flower arrangement"). The Japanese, in other words, traditionally have been minutely purposeful in their conduct and demeanor. They seem to know that a very slight action can result in extraordinary results, if done at the right time and right method. Each act has some underlying intention, incrementally linking to the overall purpose and desired outcome.

Intricate purpose

Is there a distinction between *having* a purpose and *serving* or *fulfilling* a purpose? Does a tree have a "purpose" in growing skyward or a stream in flowing downhill? Do we always understand our purpose in doing something or do we sometimes only later find that heretofore unspecified purpose? There are some things that clearly do not require forethought. Breathing, for example, is always purposeful despite the fact we are minimally intentional about it. Work also serves some purpose although we do not usually bring it to mind when we are going to and from our workplace (Smullyan, 1977, pp. 52-56).

For still other behaviors, we can assign no reason at all. We sometimes catch ourselves, for example, doodling or fidgeting. It is not important to unravel the reasons "underneath" these offbeat behaviors. Smullyan (1977) thus deplores the attitude that a person should always have a purpose for what they are doing. Having a purpose obviously can itself serve a useful purpose, just as "purposeless" activity sometimes serves a noteworthy end. In other words, we may not discern the overall or long-term meaningfulness of every action, but productive behavior does not rely on first idealizing some worthwhile goal.

Finding a sense of purpose in life, moreover, does not always include *feeling* purposeful. Satisfaction results from what we actually do. If we are feeling useless, it is time to embark on doing something useful. To do anything well is its own purposefulness. *The meaning of life is to live it.*

> The Tao has no purpose.
> And for this reason fulfills
> all its purposes admirably.
>   (Lao-tzu in Smullyan, 1977, p. 52)

As Helen Keller (1880-1968), the inimitable advocate for the deaf and blind, wrote, she longed to accomplish a great and noble task but her chief duty was to accomplish humble tasks as though they were great and noble. Keller herself received, at the age of seven, a humbling lesson from her doggedly patient teacher, Anne Mansfield Sullivan. This was Keller's resurrection from the whist, dark world in which she had lived:

> Someone was drawing water and my teacher placed my hand under the spout. As the cool stream gushed over one hand she spelled into the other the word water, first slowly, then rapidly. I stood still, my whole attention fixed upon the motions of her fingers . . . I knew then that "w-a-t-e-r"

meant the wonderful cool something that was flowing over my hand. That living word awakened my soul, gave it light, hope, joy, set it free! There would be barriers still, it is true, but barriers that could in time be swept away.

(Keller, 1903/2003)

Frankl (1955) reaffirms that the struggle of life keeps us in "suspense" because the meaning of life depends upon whether or not we fulfill the demands placed upon us by our tasks (p. 87). As Nakamura (2004) reports, not only inexperienced adolescents but also middle-aged adults, even after their neurotic symptoms are relieved, become "stranded." They stand motionless, vacantly wondering which way to proceed. It is important for the therapist to support and watch their trials and errors. Morita (1928/1998) noted that knowledge of an underground mine is useless until we "tap its lode." The work of the therapist is nothing but to convey the message that to hit a "vein" (meaning in life), the patient must first "strike a pickax" (take action) (p. 119).

Jianlin (2004) explains that in seeking a way (out of suffering) we must "avoid having a big goal and hope to have a great success." It is more useful to "have good feedback and efficacy in the short-term." Lofty goals are gained by methodic, cumulative actions. We reach the top of the ladder by navigating each intervening rung. It is feckless to aspire to the uppermost rung while tottering on the lowest. Likewise, our life purpose becomes more transparent as we immerse ourselves in meeting the tangible needs of the moment. Our lives become meaningful by "laddering" through many accomplishments. *We do not wait for purpose; purpose waits for us.*

Seikaku ha kodo niyotte kawaru.

Our character is changed by our behavior.

(Hasegawa, 1993, p. 16)

Moritists, therefore, do not command what purposes to have; they only admonish to "be purposeful." *Mokuteki hon'i* ("Hold firm to your purpose")! The natural life force within all of us carries us to a gratifying life, if we do not impede or oppose it through inattention and self-centeredness. The nearer we become to the integrity of our true natural self, the meaning of life becomes more apparent. Even those who are suicidal want to stop the pain *in* their lives, the private screams of the life they are *now experiencing*, but not their complete living. Not knowing how to live, they misguidedly relinquish whether to live. As we begin focusing on the rightful manner of being, we begin learning the "why" of living. Maturity comes through *anything* we attempt to do well. A sense of purposefulness inevitably follows.

OCD love

Those that suffer from obsessive-compulsive disorders (OCD) overrely upon invariable behaviors and flat attention. They excessively repeat the "controlled" aspects of their lives to overcompensate for those they believe they cannot manage. They are driven but not "purpose-driven." In the 1998 film, *As Good as It Gets*, for example, the curmudgeon, Melvin Udall, harbors a host of obsessions-compulsions. These include ritualistic door locking and hand washing, as well as indefatigable nastiness toward his neighbors. Melvin is unashamedly and unbendingly phobic in his avoidance of anything unclean, out-of-place, or bothersome. Life must conform to *his* demanding exactness. He shows no diffidence to the needs or reactions of others.

Carol Connelly is a waitress at the restaurant where Melvin habitually dines. Melvin anoints Carol, a single mom with a chronically asthmatic young son, as the only one solicitous enough to serve him. In actuality, Carol barely tolerates him as a customer. Melvin's fixations and heartlessness — incongruously, he is a successful romance novelist! — are later disrupted by the eventual refusal of Carol to cater any longer to his alienating eccentricities. Melvin thereupon realizes that he has fallen in love with Carol, and is no longer dispassionate about the negativity of his behavior.

One afternoon, as Melvin approaches his apartment's front door to depart for Carol's home, he is startled that, for the very first time, he had not programmatically locked and re-locked the door five times (no more and no less). He had been so preoccupied with the prospect of "losing" Carol (an aftereffect of his desire for love) that he had (momentarily) lost his compulsion (cf. Zhang & Cui, 2004). Melvin's OCD was aimless. He now had a more intentional way to live, because love is a most wondrous emotion *and* incomparable purpose (cf. Peck, 2002).

Merging Currents: We become purposeful by drawing on our natural energy.

Chapter 3

Morita Life Principle Three
Energy

"Life flows from being natural"

First return to your own real nature and you can see in every sentient being the existence of a life force and the desire for development and growth. It is an undeniable force.

Shoma Morita
(Kondo, 1975, p. 253)

Source of the Hudson

On my first visit to upstate New York, I marveled at the mighty run of the Hudson River as my friend drove us from Albany to her home in Kingston. I had lived in the Hawaiian Islands for many years and had forgotten how a major river can dominate and shape the landscape through which it flows. Everything is still-life compared to a river (Palmer, 2006, p. 41). As we traveled through rustic villages and bucolic towns along the banks of the Hudson, the force of this imposing river captivated me. Later, I asked several of my friends, gathered at a housewarming, where was the source of the Hudson. Hudson Bay? Troy? Skylarville? No one seemed to be certain.

I soon realized that my question was patently naive. I had yielded to the instinct to trace the river to its source to partially "lessen its mystery" (Herendeen, 1986, p. 11). The river, however, is a dynamic force that is elusive to annotate or typecast. A tree, stone, or mountain is relatively inert and can be facilely portrayed. The river, however, constantly moves in time and space—from source to outlet to source—defying precise definition of what is a river and when is a river (Herendeen, 1986, p. 5). As Heraclitus (540-480 BC) observed, "We cannot step into the same river twice." The Hudson is really a massive union of infinite droplets of rain and runoffs from snow melt, fed from myriad mountain ridges and valleys, converging into rivulets and gullies, then into emergent streams. The imperceptible onset of the Hudson River could be bickered about but its pure presence cannot be disputed. In the same manner, we can philosophically debate and fervently disagree on the origin (or destiny) of human life itself—ordained or evolutionary, fiat or happenstance—but yet we all must consent to its sheer reality. *Life is its own explanation and justification.*

Flowing water is the earth's great animator (Palmer, 2006, p. 41). It is the restless child of cyclical evaporation, condensation, and precipitation—a force without pin-point beginning or end relentlessly pulled by gravity downward and forward. In its journey, the river makes many turns and assumes many forms: stateliness or swiftness, stiletto tempo or rolling deluge. Even forced respite behind formidable dams, however, cannot halt its nimble force as it metamorphoses into electrical power or jettisons through spillways. Eventually and assuredly, the river arrives at its providence. As Lineen (1999) makes vivid, the passage of the Ganges from her birth in a Himalayan spring, across the vast North Indian plains, and to her death in the Bay of Bengal where she merges with the ocean is the "life of a goddess." By bathing at Haridwar where the goddess comes of age, the faithful hope to "cleanse their souls with her youthful purity while simultaneously absorbing her maturing spiritual energy" (p. 66).

Grow with the flow

The life of a river is never tame. Its flow is not flat, neat, or straight. Serendipitous, uneven terrain plunders the river's course. Our lives uniformly are a "whitewater world" (cf. Covey, 2000) where we paddle — feverish and apprehensive — through surprises, upheavals, cuts, and curves. As "river runners," we may periodically feel nervously poised on the brink of a watery precipice that constitutes a "big drop." Nash and Collins (1989), for example, write about being bowled over by the labyrinth of canyons lacing the Colorado Plateau. Of these, Cataract Canyon is the most "deceptive and devious." Above are the placid waters of the Green and Colorado rivers that lure the unsuspecting with an unwarranted confidence. The serenity belies the turbulence just ahead of the biggest cumulative drop along any stretch of the Colorado. During thunderstorms on the dry plateau above, the runoff will plunge over the cliffs in dramatic waterfalls tinted with vermillion from the reddened desert soil. The river swells between the canyon walls to three contiguous, hellacious rapids known fittingly as "Satan's Gut" (pp. 77-78).

Life may take a random "wicked drop" or "evil turn," but there is an innate intelligence within all of us that *always* strives for and pulls us to optimum health (cf. Murray & Pizzorno, 1991). This intrinsic life energy (*sei no yokubo*) fuels our instinct for physical and psychological safety, need to relate to others, and desire to live a life of meaning. The Japanese concept of life is not that of a machine that can function efficiently or break down. Life is an organic process in constant exchange with the environment (Kirmayer, 2002).

Although there are countless rivers of geographical and social variety, they all share in the unifying characteristic of water energy. In the same manner, both healthy and neurotic individuals are alike motivated by the self-actualizing tendency. The neurotic is not inherently different from a healthy person. Morita (Koga, 1967, p. 75) therefore preferred the term *shinkeishitsu* for neurosis rather than *shinkeishitsu-sho*. *Sho* is a Chinese character used in the Japanese language to denote "disease." Neurosis is not a sickness but a *phase of growth leading to a fuller use of capacities*.

As Kondo (1975) further explains, human potential is the same in all persons. The *shinkeishitsu* person is governed by the same pattern of thinking, feeling, and acting as well as experiences the same kind of conflicts, problems, and anxieties as others. The difference lies not in quality but quantity: the amount of *sei no yokubo* is not uniform in intensity among individuals (p. 250). Koga (1967) writes that *sei no yokubo* varies with each individual just as appetite, sexual desire, and desire to sleep vary (p. 77). Some of us aspire to do our utmost to live well. We engage life with irrepressible exuberance, not letting even pain and setback intimidate us (cf. Redfield Jamison, 2004). Others of us are less energetic and more restrained. Our risks are measured and our adventures are docile. Probing for "reasons" for this disparity is valueless. It is simply and candidly observed. Our life difficulties do not stem from this base difference but the thwarting of the life energy to improve ourselves: *ki ga fusagu* ("vital energy is blocked or clogged") or *ki ga meiru* (energy is leaky) (Kora, 1990).

The *stronger* is our *sei no yokubo*, the *increased* likelihood that we will suffer in life. This is because the inescapable gap between the ideal and the real gives rise to mental conflict. When we expect more of ourselves and others, the threat and effect of discordance grows. By analogy, the stronger the iron coil the more tension is generated when it is pressed down. Those who suffer the most can be the most accomplished and successful because of their drive for advancement. The most problem-ridden have the innateness to be superior if their *sei no yokubo* can be released from being compressed by misdirection of attention and oppressed by hypersensitive awareness of disadvantages and shortcomings. *Overattention to our personal weaknesses burns up valuable life energy.*

Natural spontaneity

In 1910, the Montessori system of childhood education was introduced into Japan from Italy, and exerted a major influence on Morita's view of natural life energy (Azuma, 2004). Montessori advocates that spontaneous activity is highly effective in fostering education in children, because it allows them to be free and self-reliant (Morita, 1928/1998, p. 98). This does not mean giving children the license to impulsively act out. Morita noticed that the Montessori environment includes normal learning materials, supplies, playthings, and books, but there is no unyielding schedule or instructional format. Montessori teachers encourage children to exhibit their natural curiosity and exploration. As we age into adulthood we seem less able to improvise, and begin limiting ourselves to "scripts" of stereotyped responses (Corey, 2008, p.

187). Unlike adults, children have a native "playfulness": they romp from one activity to the next.

Early in his psychiatric practice, Morita began treating small groups of mildly retarded adolescents in his home to observe them in daily living. He left the children alone to do whatever they chose. The children quickly became bored while waiting and soon bounded into action. *Sei no yokubo* is epitomized by the adaptability, immersion, and abilities displayed by *unimpeded* children. As the spunky 14-year-old Velvet Brown is immortalized in *National Velvet* (Bagnold, 1935): "How can there be so many currents in such a little puddle!"

Unfortunately, many adults squander away this energy through inflexible thinking, self-absorption, and behavioral passivity. The *shinkeishitsu* person, Morita (1928/1998) explained, will become overwhelmed by the anticipatory desire for success, begin to think about the difficulty of the task, and focus on the fear of failure (p. 45). It would seem preferable to deal with potentially big problems before they became big. A sapling is easy to affect but a mature tree is not (Loy, 1985, p. 76). The neurotic person, however, becomes incapable of even starting the task and lapses into idleness.

Kapleau (1967) instructs that we must unlock rigid notions of how things ought to be. Productivity requires energy and energy flows most freely in those who are able to adapt easily to new obstacles and changing conditions. Rigidity, on the other hand, makes conflict inevitable and the resulting frustration saps our energies and interferes with a whole hearted effort (p. 11). Lao-tzu (604-531 BC) likewise portends: "The stiff and unbending is the disciple of death." Pine branches break off under the weight of heavy snow fall. The bending willow, however, can drop its burden and spring up again (Loy, 1985, p. 76). Ishiyama's (1998) term for the condition that prevents us from seeing past the curtains of excessive anxieties, phobias, and neuroses is "dogmatic self-containment."

Dogmatic self-containment

The late Bruce Lee, the greatest martial artist of the modern era, taught his pupils the philosophy of "No way as way. No limitation as limitation." There is no *single* response to an aggressive, physical threat (or life challenge). We must be pliable, "ready but not tense, not thinking yet not dreaming." Change with change for the "softest thing cannot be snapped" (Lee, 1975, p. 203). We also must complement not succumb to our opponent's force and fighting style (or adversarial event), compensating according to the circumstances *as they present themselves*. To thrust when a thrust is not needed is wasteful. To lunge when a lunge leaves us defenseless is foolhardy.

Lee developed Jeet Kune Do ("the way of the intercepting fist") as a method to free the natural flow of movement according to one's own physical attributes and acquired skills. Lee himself was no more than 5 feet 8 inches tall and weighed less than 150 pounds. He was near-sighted and his right leg was one inch shorter than his left. He was a most formidable martial artist, however, because he adapted to his limitations and capitalized on his strengths. Lee termed this "effortless effort." Instead of trying to do everything well, we are to do those things perfectly of which we are capable (Hyams, 1979, pp. 35-36). The key to powerful combat and life is to honestly express your self without conformity to some artificial style or restriction to an idealistic mindset (Lee, 1975, p. 17).

The capacity to free our natural power is illustrated in the case of "Rachel," a young client who had formed a desperate dependence on psychotropic medication (Ogawa, 1997). Rachel's psychiatrist had sternly warned her that she was on the verge of yet another hospitalization in a strait jacket should she stray from treatment. Fearful of triggering a relapse, Rachel curbed her social activities and work responsibilities to tend to her all-consuming illness. She was like a shipwrecked sailor bobbing on the roiling sea, clinging fiercely to her life preserver (*kyūmeigu*).

When Rachel was subsequently referred to me for counseling, she was distressed that her life was "going nowhere." She felt "adrift at the mercy of capricious winds and currents," ruled by painful self-doubt and the dwindling expectations of her family. Rachel's inclination was to discontinue her medication altogether, believing that it severely dampened her motivation and drive to do much of anything. She decided she would rather "flail" in her life than become flotsam in the "placid sea of nothingness." Pinker (2004) argues that tweaking the brain with drugs may sometimes be the solenoid to jump-start the machinery that we call the will. Rachel was obviously "willing" to live better, but lacked the specifics as to how to do so.

Rachel started anew with modest steps (figuratively, she was a "novice swimmer"). The dosage of her medication, for example, was adjusted — rather than wholesale discarded — in consultation with her treating psychiatrist, because pharmacotherapy can play an important role in conjunction with Morita therapy (Nakamura, 2004; Mashino, 2004). Many Japanese psychiatrists were trained in the biologically-oriented and medication-focused German neuropsychiatry that was first introduced into Japan in the early 1900s. Morita's perspective, however, is that constitution-based disorders are modifiable through disciplined practice (Kirmayer, 2002, pp. 300, 317). Any medication that debilitates this capacity for development is considered more damaging than helpful. The taking of a pill (*kusuri*) to feel better is implicitly a moral choice.

Rachel abandoned "splashing about" and begin intently practicing deliberate actions ("flutter kicks") to develop the skills and responsibility for doing more and more. She devoted her energies toward the life *she* wanted, such as obtaining a college degree. One single task ("stroke") at a time (e.g., applying to college and enrolling in classes) brought her steadily closer to this achievement. Rachel progressed from "sinking" in self-deprecation and anguish (dogmatic self-containment) to "free-styling" with buoyant spirit and self-trust (natural openness).

Shizen

Respecting nature (*shizen*) and obeying natural life processes have been key themes of Japanese history. The Japanese have resisted wholly objectifying nature as occurs in the natural sciences (botany, zoology, etc.) and Western philosophy. Nature is not "a thing of itself" to be enumerated or rationalized. Although the lives of modern, urbanized Japanese are suffused with artificial and synthetic trappings, they remain receptive to the influences of nature. Nature has a central bearing on human life, and thus is not seen as existing apart from humans and society. Nature is not only the means of survival but also the means to liberating and aesthetic experience (Narazaki, 1970, p. 8). The Japanese, accordingly, find their chief pleasure in the contemplation of oneness with nature.

The grand teamaster Rikyū (1522-1591), for example, was said to have scattered a few leaves over a garden path that had recently been swept in order to give it a natural look and to emphasize the beauty of natural process (Keene, 1989, p. 134). Japanese gardens are seldom symmetrical or manicured with precision-bordered rows. Plantings, stones, and water features are placed to evoke natural settings. The Japanese do not attempt to delineate and subjugate nature. In Japanese ink painting, a few brush strokes serve to suggest whole mountain ranges, or a single stroke to imply a stalk of bamboo. Keene (1989) explains that a mountain painted in green can never be any other color, but a mountain whose outlines are given with a few strokes of black ink can be *any* color (p. 131).

The term *kācho fugetsu* represents this refined oneness with nature. *Kācho* is literally "flowers and birds" or "wind and moon" (Narazaki, 1970, p. 7). The flowers and birds or other natural phenomena are never extolled as objects of beauty in their own right, but are invested with human yearnings, emotions, or ideas. Nature changes, yet is eternal. The Japanese are drawn to appreciate life more as they follow the natural grace of impermanence above the "contrived elegance" of man (Narazaki, 1970, p. 9). There is hence a particular fondness for ritualizing the changing of the seasons. There is plum blossom viewing that heralds the approach of spring; cherry blossom in early April; lotuses in summer; moon viewing, maple viewing, and chrysanthemum viewing in autumn; and snow viewing in winter. Various other natural phenomena, such as waterfalls or the changing tide, can also be occasions for special excursions (Narazaki, 1970, p. 9).

The Japanese are particularly attracted to cherry blossoms not as much for their lustrous beauty but their perishability (Keene, 1989). Cherry blossoms fall after a brief three days of flowering. Delicate cherry blossom trees are planted everywhere even in parts of Japan where the climate is scarcely hospitable. Human life, too, is ethereal. Kenkō (1283-1350) writes:

> If man were never to fade away like the dews of Adashino, never to vanish like the smoke over Toribeyama, but lingered on forever in this world, how things would lose their power to move us! The most precious thing in life is its uncertainty.
> (Keene, 1989, p. 134)

Like the "flower rafts" of cherry blossom petals that have fallen into the river and are carried along in clusters, nature to the Japanese is the ultimate home and life a temporary lodging (Narazaki, 1970, pp. 9-10). To live with this naturalness of being includes freeing the natural reactions of the mind and body to what is experienced in daily living (Kitanishi & Mori, 1995, p. 246). The regular round of seasons mirrors the daily birth and death of thoughts, emotions, and vitality. To live naturally is to make nature an integral part of our lives *and* our lives an integral part of nature.

Healing energy

Everything is a form of energy. Even matter we deem "rock solid" is a dynamic bundle. The more we tap into our own strength and plug it into surrounding energy currents, the more we experience life's harmonizing power. Regrettably, in our prevailing culture, our minds and bodies seem most vigilant when we're angry, upset, afraid, or worried. Inflammatory hormones, brain chemicals, and other acute physiological responses to these states may be useful in measured bursts. "Fight or flight," however, is a reactive survival mechanism more than a long-term beach resort for wellbeing. In unresolved, chronic stress our immune system suffers harmful, sometimes fatal, consequences, including headaches, rashes, infertility, digestive ailments, cancer, and heart attacks.

Heredity, of course, plays a role in being stress-prone and stress-resilient. Nonetheless, how we style our lives makes a critical difference. It partially determines how we behave when we are victimized and roughed up. The pass-through is whether or not we concentrate our energy in a *healing* direction (cf. Ornish, 1999). Mindfulness meditation, for example, has been verified to produce demonstrable effects on brain and immune function (Davidson, Kabat-Zinn, Schumacher, Rosenkranz, Muller, Santorelli, Urbanowski, Harrington, Bonus, & Sheridan, 2003). How we employ our inborn energy affects our personal health, relationships, and lifework. Misdirected or misplaced, this energy becomes injurious and debilitating. In Morita's words (1928/1998, p. 19), it is only "artificial schemes" to push back the water of Kyoto's Kamo River that prevents us from living powerfully. Our true nature can be *trusted* because it is not an alkaline crawl toward a desiccated flat.

D. T. Suzuki (1991) similarly teaches that our innate energies impel our faculty for happiness and love.

Yamato Damashii

Yamato is what the Japanese formerly designated their homeland. *Yamato Damashii* ("spirit of Japan") refers to extraordinary perseverance in the face of all obstacles (Lafayette De Mente, 1997, p. 23). This spirit ("guts") is considered the key to success in any endeavor, even more than talent itself. The Japanese will generally work harder and longer, undertaking any task whether or not they know anything about it. They simply never give up, sacrificing themselves to ruin if necessary, because failure to be tenacious in the pursuit of a sanctioned task is judged to be exceedingly shameful. *Karoshi* ("death by overwork") is thus a real danger for the Japanese, especially males whose *ikigai* ("reason for living") tends to be their work. Economic downturns or career reversals subject these men to depression and suicide (Kirmayer, 2002, p. 307). Retirement, to be duly honored, must also be seen not as "joblessness" but an earned accomplishment.

The steadfast manner that the Japanese go about their lives is not principally for personal gain but for some group interest: family, clan, village, or nation (Kirmayer, 2002, p. 306). The business culture of Japan, for example, stakes itself on the *kaizen* ("improvement") mind, the unending drive to improve the *company's* position and not the aggrandizement of a high ranking officer or employee. The company is a family or village of co-workers. Open offices without cubicles, consensus-building, and organizational creed buttress the norm of shared purpose. Successes are attributed to the pool of dedicated work and shortfalls to individuals not meeting their output targets (Fackler, 2007).

One of the mythological stories of the creation of the Japanese islands is *Susano'o no Mikoto,* the god of the sea and storms. Susano'o had a long-standing rivalry with his sister, Amaterasu, the goddess of the sun. The siblings challenged one another to transform a personal object of the other's into human form. Amaterasu created three women from Susano'o's sword while he created five men from her necklace. Enraged by Amaterasu's claim that the men were now hers because they were born of her necklace, Susano'o destroyed her rice fields, hurled a flayed pony at her loom, and killed one of her attendants. Amaterasu fled into Ame-no-Iwata, the "heavenly rock cave," hiding the sun for a long period of time. Susano'o was punished for his fury by being banished from heaven.

The Japanese abhor arrogant, thoughtless, and selfish behavior. Such behavior brings about *haji* ("shame") and a soiling of *meiyo* ("personal dignity"). The Japanese are very sensitive to this type of chastisement, but must not be so collared to conformity that they countermand their "inner promptings" and become "empty shells of pretense" (cf. Corey, 2008, p. 229). There is a fine line between freeing one's energy to accomplish much and being overly self-assertive. A "fighting spirit" is admired as long as it is not chiefly self-serving. Self-actualization is therefore the conversion of individual potential into social influence.

Merging Currents: We benefit most from the momentum of our natural energy by learning to live fully in the present.

Chapter 4

Morita Life Principle Four
Moments

"Life flows from being present"

Satori (enlightenment) and "correct" ideation are obtained by experientially knowing the reality of daily life that is right before one's eyes.
Shoma Morita
(1928/1998, p. 78)

Momentum

Our lives consist of a virtual tide of moments. If we allow each of these moments to instill its particular meaningfulness, we acquire the *moment*um of life's natural flow. What happens now, in this very moment, influences what happens next (cf. Kabat-Zinn, 1994). *This* moment must be lived well or the experience of *every* moment is potentially lost. In the Zen saying: "One moment, one encounter" (*ichigo-ichi'e*). Each moment occurs once in a lifetime. This is what Ives (1992, p. 36) refers to as the full use, economic and moral, of everything that comes our way. What becomes the "opportune" or "decisive" moments to shape our lives can only emanate from not taking *any* moment for granted.

Director-writer Hirokazu Kore-eda depicts the poignant timelessness of moments in the 1998 Japanese film, *After Life*. The newly deceased file one-by-one into a drab office in the hereafter to be "processed" by caseworkers. The caseworkers explain that within the next several days the deceased must extract a single, precious life moment. This incomparable moment will then be recited to the caseworkers, who will arrange for it to be faithfully recreated on film with appropriate props, sets, and costumes. Instantaneously, after viewing the completed film in a private theater, the deceased will pass into eternity with *only* that solitary memory! The alternative to making such a choice is a vacuous existence with no memory of anyone or anything from one's life. To some, this alternative seems preferable because of the palpable weight of regrets, indiscretion, or wrongdoing. To forget in death bestows a sardonic but beneficent ending to a sense of uselessness and futility.

Confronted with this task, an elderly gentleman is dismayed because he deems his life to have been featureless: an insipid career, nondescript marriage, and unimaginative hobbies. The caseworkers prod him to study their videotape archive of his life in order to aid his reflection. The man anguishes for days over the unfolding scenes. In time, he arrives at the awkward first meeting with his future wife. He reminisces on her sympathy toward his bumbling, timid attempts at speaking. Seemingly unaffected by his inelegance, she introduces the subject of favorite films. Their conversation thereafter becomes more animated and delightful. The man later pairs this scene with one 40 years later when he is sitting with his wife on a park bench not long before her death. They speak fondly to one another about their earliest encounter and subsequent long marriage. This moment of devotion will now accompany this husband forevermore.

A young woman giddily decides that an amusement park ride is her crowning instance. Teenagers, she advertises, crave wild thrills to ward off loneliness and insecurity. Days after, however, the young woman discards her impetuous choice of thundering roller coasters. Her thoughts have turned to a wintry night when she is a child. She is glancing up at her mother quietly sitting on the sofa. Without fuss, she crawls onto her mother's lap to nestle in the softness and warmth. The bliss of mother and child is eternal.

A middle-aged man boasts of his erotic conquests, exclaiming to the caseworkers that any man would pick ecstasy. He breathlessly recounts his many fatuous trysts. On the evening before a final decision, a different moment comes to light: a tearful father at his daughter's wedding. He is standing in the reception hall, feelings of immense joy and painful separation welling within him. At an instant, his eyes coincidentally meet the affectionate wink of his daughter from across the room. This serendipitous moment becomes far more cherished than all the dalliances.

After Life probes us with this question: "What moment would we ourselves choose?" This elicits a quandary: How can we choose just one? It also whets our sensibilities that *any* moment — even if *presumably* slight — may be, in the *last accounting*, the most endearing. As Millman (1992) writes, we find a new relationship with life when we treat every moment as "sacred." It is not what we get *from* each moment, but what we bring *to* it. We make each moment count (p. xvi).

One of the most heartrending scenes in *After Life* is the persistent refusal of one of the caseworkers to search for her own unique memory. Everyone she has ever known has already died and passed through, but no one has chosen her as an everlasting memory. She had yearned to be *inochi no onjin* ("most precious benefactress") to someone in her lifetime. Now she remains in the purgatory of disgrace and disaffection, never having been the source of anyone's unsurpassable moment of love or meaning.

Not knowing what happens next

Gilda Radner was the icon of outlandish comedic characters on the popular television show, *Saturday Night Live*. Her stand-up performances were punctuated with wacky caricatures that tickled our hearts and rattled our funny bones. Radner's untimely death from *un*funny ovarian cancer left a terrible frown upon our lives. Her contemplative style and words, however, during the course of her dying have made a most enduring punch-line. Radner (2000) admitted that she wanted a perfect ending to her life but learned that "some poems don't rhyme" and what happens the very next moment is a mystery. The goal is to live a productive life in the midst of ambiguity.

This present moment is the one to live well. Its "expansive effect," as ciphered by Yasutani-roshi (Kapleau, 1967), is the dot in the intersection of the horizontal line of "beginningless past and endless future" and the vertical line of "limitless space." The present moment embraces all of these dimensions (p. 15). If we are missing plenty of these moments, we are then missing a lot of life! Kabat-Zinn (1994) states that *this* moment is the only time that we have in which to live, grow, feel, and change. We need to take precautions against the "incredible pull of the Scylla and Charybdis of past and future," and the dreamworld they offer us in place of our lives (p. xv).

Living in the moment, however, should not be mistaken for living *for* the moment. "For the moment" means that no other moment counts: we are perpetually swayed by impulse and tossed by whim, storming into whatever grabs our instant fancy. There is little regard for consequences because tomorrow does not matter. We are like rockets wildly blasting off into unknown orbit! The only purpose of living for the moment, consequently, is to place all purposes at the highest risk. Every life purpose would succumb to this haphazard push and pull of superficial beckoning, making our lives as shallow and obscure as a muddy puddle!

"In the moment" is the opposite. Every moment has some significance in preventing us from violating our commitments. We make the most of these moments in order to be consistent and purposeful. Benoit Lecomte of Austin, Texas, for example, set out on July 16, 1998 from Cape Cod to be the first person to swim across the Atlantic Ocean (Phillips, 1998). His scant equipment consisted of mask, fins, snorkel, two layers of wet suit, and electronic shark repellant. Swimming 40-50 miles a day, accompanied by a single escort boat, Lecomte persisted through frigid seas, fierce winds, towering swells, and perpetual taste of salt water in his mouth. Monotony, loneliness, and nausea almost forced him to quit midway. But Lecomte, who conceived of the swim as a way to honor his father who had died of colon cancer at age 49, stubbornly kept to his adopted rule of never thinking about the next day, hour, or minute. His life and purpose at peril, Lecomte could not abandon his focus on one efficient stroke and economical breath at a time. Seventy-three days and 3,700 miles after he plunged into the Atlantic, Lecomte came ashore in Quiberon, France, into the arms of his awaiting fiancée.

Firewood never becomes ashes

In a centuries-old Japanese farmhouse (*minka*) sequestered in a remote hillside of tea bush terraces, a group of Americans and Japanese gathered in the mid-1980s to study Morita therapy. Each one of us was presented a personal *koan* (Zen riddle) to contemplate and unravel. A *koan* is a dense and opaque puzzle, the solving of which is meant to provoke sudden enlightenment (*kensho*). The perplexity of a *koan* reveals the "inherent incompleteness" of rational solution and intellectual banter to discover truth. Only when exhausted by the rejection of facile answers, does the seeker benefit from the reorganization of consciousness and experience (Kirmayer, 2002, p. 210). Examples of *koans* include: "Use your spade which is in your empty hands." "Walk while riding on a donkey." "Let me hear the sound of one hand clapping." These logical impossibilities or paradoxical propositions, are meant to "tax the intellect" and "wake up the totality of our being" (Suzuki, Fromme, & DeMartino, 1963, p. 51). The intellectual blind alley to which we are driven is like "the silver mountain" or "the iron wall" standing right in front of us. The *whole of our being* is needed to effect a penetration (p. 50).

My consigned *koan* was "Firewood never becomes ashes." Firewood, I reasoned, does become ashes when burned. How can it *never* become ashes when consumed? For days, I periodically revisited the *koan* during silent meditation, forest walks, and purifying soaks in the *furo* ("Japanese-style bath tub"). One evening, while thoroughly engaged in stoking the flames of the open pit on which we cooked our meals, I was startled that the meaning of the *koan* flared before me. The *process* of burning was clearly present as I intently fanned the flames. Was my attention, however, to the burning itself replacing "appreciation" of the individual elements: wood pieces, embers, and coal? Firewood is now *only* firewood, and ashes are now *only* ashes. *Now* firewood, *now* ashes. The *present* moment is the most critical and is whole and complete in itself.

It is not that the past and future are irrelevant; it is that they receive their content from the present. When we mull, grieve, or rejoice over the past, it is from the perspective of the present. Linus, Charles Schultz's thumb-sucking cartoon philosopher in *Peanuts*, clenches his ever-present "security blanket" and bemoans his anxiety about the future. Charlie Brown replies, "I'm still hoping that yesterday will get better!" It actually can get better if we allow the present to take hold, thus removing the power of the hoary past to harm us. The meaning of the past revises in the light of final outcomes. As Shuster (2004) narrates, it is like the time we lost the love of our life, the one we hoped to marry, because of a foolish bit of selfishness or pride. It was our own fault that the person we cared about most in life was now gone forever. But time passed — lonely time — then the impossible thing happened, and we met the person more right for us and the past looked different. In fact, it was different, because "the way it affected the present has become different" (p. 22).

Moreover, the only way our everyday prospects come into sterling fruition is through the concerted actions of today. Tomorrow, the present becomes the past. Similarly, the future has its birth in current deeds. We create both an honorable past and a worthy future by living well in the present. A Chinese proverb thereby exhorts: "Distant water cannot extinguish a nearby fire" (Char, 1970, p. 29). Wistful remorse, disparaging self-blame, or flimsy excuses for what might have been are far less productive than doing what *now* needs to be done in the midst of present reality. *We can look back but never go back.*

Ashes were once firewood. These very same ashes eventually become the nourishment for subsequent tree growth, which thereafter becomes new firewood. There is a "bi-directional cycle of life": from the present to the past *and* from the present to the future. It is when we become messily mired in the past or gravely worried about the future that we fail to live with real strength. Whatever our errant past or elusive future, the present does not offer compromise to do less or do less well. Each new moment liberates us to do better than we have and to start afresh on our future. As Morita (Ohara, 1990, p. 61) wrote, "*Hi-ni arata-ni mata hi-ni arata-ni*" ("Each day is a new day"). No matter what our situation or hurdle, the control and responsibility to flourish happens in only one place: what we do with our lives *right now.*

Breathing

Those who suffer from chronic emphysema, asthma, pneumonia, or other serious pulmonary diseases are guileless about banking on each breath taken. If you have had your wind knocked out by an abrupt blow to the chest, or have nearly died from drowning or suffocation, you have also been summoned: breathing takes precedence over any other issue or concern. Later will not exist if we do not breathe *now.* Just as momentary cessation of breathing or labored gasping for air recalls the fragility of life, attention to and appreciation of breathing also opens the "passageway to the immediate."

Our breathing is an integrating rhythm that physically, mentally, and emotionally brings us back to center. As Iyengar (2002) illuminates, our mind fluctuates in a split second, never standing still as it whizzes back and forth. In contrast, breathing—though it can pause for moments of retention—has only one path: inhalation and exhalation. Controlling our breathing and observing its regularity, accordingly, brings the consciousness to stillness so that the "soul pervades the entire body" (p. 5).

Now is who I am

Delancey Street Foundation is a residential education center, founded in 1971, where former criminals and homeless learn to forge new lives. It has been called the most successful rehabilitation project in the United States. Mimi Silbert, the program's founder, challenges addicts and ex-felons to focus on not what they were but what they are becoming. As Cobb (1975) confirms, "The one who simply holds onto the past and repeats it . . . merely joins it in death" (p. 243). In Eastern thought, notwithstanding, unless this pull toward the "ought" (what could and should be) is balanced by a companion sense of what *is*, life becomes "forward heavy" (cf. Kapleau, 1967, p. xiii.). Theodore Isaac Rubin (1975), author of *Compassion and Self-hate*, cautions:

> I do not permit goals, plans and ambitions to impoverish, let alone destroy, any aspect of who I am currently. Utmost respect for who I am must precede and take precedence over who I may become. The same is true of who I have been.
>
> (p. 200).

Overinvestment in outcomes can distract us from being fully empowered in our present choices and actions. Siddhartha said, "Finding means: to be free, to be receptive, to have no goal . . . for in striving towards your goal, you do not see many things that are under your nose." Having no goal does not mean being without purpose. It means that when goals themselves are the cynosure of attention rather than the performance of some concrete activity central to reaching that goal, we will not arrive at what we desire. *Possibility becomes actuality by participating in the actual.* As a young father and Morita group member relates:

Recently we had a baby. The struggles and anticipation throughout the labor and delivery was soon beyond us and we eagerly awaited the future hopes of parenthood . . .
I would catch myself many times overthinking and dreaming about our baby past the diaper stage, walking, talking and amusing us with her newly acquired antics. The possibilities of what we could do to interest her in music, art, reading and math soon entertained my thoughts . . . .
(But) this tendency of subtle escaping can be damaging for both parents and child. The child is pushed to accomplish the parents' dream and the parents lose the experience of seeing their child grow moment by moment.

(Christians In-Depth Fellowship, 1978, p. 2)

Just standing

Fuji-yama (Mt. Fuji) is the most revered mountain and place in Japan. Almost too perfectly shaped to be natural, its impressive symmetry makes it the most recognizable mountain on earth (Olmstead, 2006). Hokusai (1760-1849), the ukiyo-e master (paintings and wood block prints), is especially famous for his collection, *One Hundred Views of Mount Fuji*, in which he depicts the mountain from a variety of perspectives and positions in every season. The Japanese call Mt. Fuji the honorific Fuji-*san*—like a respected person. Climbing this towering 12,389 feet mountain—really hiking and walking its river of switch-backs—is a pilgrimage undertaken by anyone with good lungs and patience, including the elderly and children. Offerings are made at trailside altars for health and long life.

When the Japanese people behold Fuji-san's massive presence—Zen-like and solid—it reminds them also to be firmly grounded. Emulating Fuji-san is to practice being uncomplicatedly present in place and time. This is illustrated in the following Zen story of three men at the base of a mountain who saw a solitary man standing at the top and started discussing his purpose in being there:

One suggested, "Perhaps he is looking for a friend."
Another suggested, "Perhaps he is looking for his dog."
The third suggested, "No, maybe he is standing there to just enjoy the fresh air."

The three then climbed to the summit. One asked the man, "You have lost a friend?" The man replied, "No." The second asked, "Oh, you looking for your dog?" The man replied, "No." The third said, "Ah, so I am right! You are standing there just to enjoy the fresh air!" The man replied, "No."

The three were extremely puzzled! Finally, one said, "Then why are you standing here?" The man replied, "I am just standing here."

(Smullyan, 1977, p. 55)

* * * * * * * * * * * * * *

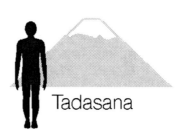

Tadasana

- *To experience your own ability to "just stand," spend a few minutes in the "Mountain Pose" (tadasana). Your difficulty or ease in doing so will help you determine your ability to center in the here and now, no matter the setting or situation.*

- *Position your feet pointed forward and slightly apart. Allow your weight to flow downward. Attend to a stationary object in the distance. Soften your eyes; do not stare. Soften your shoulders; do not tense them. Let your arms rest at your sides with your hands open and relaxed.*

- *Breathe normally. Let your thoughts and feelings come and go, not attaching to any one.*

- *Just stand. Just be.*

* * * * * * * * * * * * * *

From this moment on

A solitary stone dropped into a pool sets in motion concentric ripples, animating the waters relative to the stone's dimensions and force of entry. A pebble is barely discernible in its effect; a mass explodes the calm. Distinct moments likewise continuously enter into our lives. Each moment sends waves of energy into our daily existence. Some "perfect" moments impress us more than others. We might never want to leave these moments, retreating into them as long as possible. Others we might want to splice from our memory in toto.

Albom (1997) writes how his friend, Morrie, used to go to a church in Harvard Square every Wednesday night for something called "Dance Free." Morrie would dance to whatever music was playing, twisting and twirling, waving his arms like "a conductor on amphetamines." No one realized that he was a distinguished and typically staid university professor. Once, Morrie brought a tango tape and had it played over the speakers. He "commandeered the floor, shooting back and forth like some hot Latin lover" (p. 6). When Morrie finished his gyrations, everyone applauded. He would have stayed in that moment forever.

As Millman (1992), however, reminds us, "If life gets our attention with a serious illness, we have no alternative but to deal with it" (p. 42). After Morrie developed asthma and then Lou Gehrig's, the dancing, sadly, did stop. Nevertheless, though bedridden and weakening, he met with Albom for fourteen Tuesdays to impart hard-won lessons on life, love, and family. Morrie understood that each moment of living—to the very last—invites us to rumba, tap, or sway to its idiosyncratic metrics. We are not meant to be demure wallflowers waiting for only sunrise moments to choreograph our life spirit.

Merging Currents: As the present unfolds we must accept that we do not control everything.

Chapter 5

Morita Life Principle Five Acceptance

"Life flows from being realistic"

Sense a cold temperature as cold, experience pains and fears as they are, suffer a conflict as it torments us . . .
That is, to obey nature means to unconditionally obey the facts, the truths.

Shoma Morita
(1928/1974, p. 80)

Live as it is

The river is not afforded a glass channel. It abides by whatever it meets along its course, finding the path of *greatest simplicity* and *least amount of effort*. The river adjusts when less is too little and more is too much. The power and beauty of the river is this natural fluidity to reform and transform itself. Similarly, disclaiming the less-than-utopian state of our lives prevents us from amending to a more fulfilling one. Reality *(genjitsu)* is not always as we conjure it to be, but denial of fact is like treading water in a rushing current. As Wang (2004) avows: "Live as it is."

It is human nature to want to exercise control in life. In "primary control," the form most commonly referred to in the psychological literature (Weisz, et al., 1996, p. 64), we attempt to bring external events or environmental conditions in line with our wishes. The world is to be mastered. In "secondary control," we attempt to exert control by bringing ourselves into harmony with prevailing events and conditions in ways to make those events and conditions more rewarding or less punishing. For the Japanese, secondary control generally plays a more important role in everyday life.

Japan, for example, is within the most geologically active zone in the world. It lies atop several tectonic plates and has a jarring 1,000 earthquakes per year. The Kanto Plain where Tokyo lies is particularly defenseless. It is estimated that there is a 70% chance that a quake between 6.7 and 7.2 on the Richter Magnitude Scale will hit Tokyo or neighboring prefectures by 2030. The last time a big earthquake did so was in 1923 when the ensuing fires and crumpled buildings killed more than 100,000 citizens.

In 2004, I was visiting with the founding director of the Higa Mental Health Clinic in Tokyo and her psychiatric staff. We were discussing the application of Morita therapy across treatment populations when the building began to tremble and sway. There was instant hesitation in the group. My Japanese colleagues seem to be carefully evaluating the rumbling juggernaut in order to know what proper action to take. There was no panic displayed. Were we all worried? Of course! Soon, one of the psychologists departed to see what possible damage had been done to other parts of the building, and if the other staff members and clients were safe. The rest of us slowly resumed our conversation. We later learned that a 6.8 magnitude quake centered in Ojiya, about 160 miles northwest of Tokyo, had rocked the area. Twenty-three people were killed and 1,800 injured. The quake ripped up roads, flattened villages, and knocked one of Japan's famed bullet trains off its rails—the first time since the lauded system's inception in 1964. The tremor was the deadliest since the 7.2 magnitude quake to strike Kobe in 1995, killing more than 6,400 (Moffett, 2004).

Despite the deaths, injuries, and destruction that hemorrhage from the unrivaled force of these earthquakes—as well as the preemptory typhoons, flooding, and tsunamis—the Japanese are tenacious. They accept this ruthless reality, repair their civic infrastructure, and return to daily functions as soon as conditions allow. This does not, however, exonerate them from fortifying their buildings to strict codes, monitoring seismic precursors, and developing more efficient disaster response measures (Johnstone, 2005). Loss of life from earthquakes, for example, comes mainly from buildings collapsing. Since many of the victims are lethally trapped rather than instantly killed, their chances of survival would be much higher if they could be rescued quickly. Research also indicates that survivors of collapsed housing who are forced to relocate to public and private shelters suffer increased mental burden (Joh, 1997). The Japanese have accepted both the ominous natural disasters and the collateral responsibility to be as ready as possible.

Hibakusha

The *hibakusha* are survivors of cataclysmic events far more ruinous than any natural gamble: Hiroshima, August 6 and Nagasaki, August 9, 1945. These unprecedented and never again (thus far) replicated nuclear bombings instantaneously killed 120,000 men, women, and children and at least twice as many from the effects of being exposed to the searing and lingering radiation. Households and livelihoods were obliterated, and the political and cultural landscape inverted by these weapons of mass destruction. For many *hibakusha* the aftermath commenced a lifetime of struggle to overcome heartrending physical injury and ailments. The *hibakusha* live with the perpetual threat of delayed radiation effects and the dread that they may transmit contagions and illnesses to future offspring. Luc and Gaudriault (2005) record one survivor's ordeal:

> As a 19-year-old, Mitoya was at school when he heard a B-29 overhead. Classmates who ran to the windows to look were incinerated by the flash of the explosion. Mitoya eventually became an engineer. Two of his three children developed brain cancer; one died. He underwent an operation for stomach cancer.
>
> (p. 40)

Many *hibakusha* see radiation as perverting their blood, and have resorted to folk remedies and herbs for purging. They have also employed forced bodily elimination processes such as bleeding, vomiting, and profuse sweating to expel the poisonous pollutant. Health, regardless, is not coterminous with absence of somatic diseases. Health is also a mental and social condition. The *hibakusha* bear the psychic trauma caused by the atomic bomb (*genshibakudan*) and a society that shuns them out of fear they would contaminate others. Identified as "defiled" by other Japanese, the *hibakusha* are blotted as unmarriageable and unemployable. Many of the *hibakusha* are furthermore angered by the mistreatment they believe is meted out by insensitive medical researchers and uncaring health-care providers. For many years the long-term effects of radiation were surreptitiously deemed "harmless" by both American and Japanese authorities to help avert judgment that the bombings were inhumane acts. Sledgehammer media censorship of the after-effects reinforced the concealment of the *hibakusha*.

Still yet, many "mushroom cloud victims" have tirelessly worked against nuclear proliferation. They embody and attest to both the blasphemy of warfare and halcyon of peace. Much of our understanding of how radiation causes cancer also comes from the study of 80,000 *hibakusha*, the largest epidemiological research ever. This represents the gold standard for cancer studies (Simonite, 2005). The forsaken *hibakusha* somehow find the courage to live even as many of us are hoping to find the courage to die. They have permutated from secluded pariahs of pity and scorn to public saints of medical science and humanitarian causes.

Japan as a whole has remarkably reconstructed from the nefarious position of "A-bombed nation." Its potent economism has made it a world-wide non-militaristic force. Deadly fission did not weaken the Japanese will but roused it to establish a more prosperous homeland. Japan is not as it once was nor what it could have been. It is what it has become today. Definitions of national and individual health — learned from the Japanese experience — must ever include the effort made toward health, artful adaptability, and the strength to keep living (Ikuta, 1996). As one of the *hibakusha* offered, "The bomb is not a matter of survival; it is a matter of living" (Todeschini, 1999, p. 67).

Arugamama

We do not decide everything that life brings to us, but we are responsible for everything we bring to life! This engagement transpires in the midst of *any* reality – no matter how inconvenient, hurtful, or distasteful. Morita's term for this concession to "reality-as-it-is" is *arugamama* (Kusama, 1973). As Morita (1928/1998, p. 19) analogized, "Heat is also cool when one is in a mindless state." "Mindless state" is meeting whatever happens in life without undue preference, criticism, or contempt – the "radical acceptance of the entirety of the moment" (Dimidjian & Linehan, 2003, p. 229).

Contrariwise, when we try to avoid or manipulate reality, we invite a heightened sense of aggravation and powerlessness. It is as futile as attempting to force summer or winter to straight away pass (Matesz, 1990, p. 18). Reality-as-it-is *now*, however, is as impermanent as the temporal seasons. Where our lives are at this moment is a transition to where we could be next. This freedom to act comes from the "wide sphere of possibilities" for human behavior (Kora, 1990, p. 10). As Seelye (1977) describes, the bright thing we are after may be just around the next river bend. The bend is "prophetic" as to what may be obtained beyond. It is only when we do not heed the "language of water" that we become unimaginative and cease to explore.

Arugamama is thus not the loss but *re-channeling* of drive when there are plausible actions to assuage existing conditions. It is not *akirame*, limp submission or fateful resignation (Kora, 1990, p. 9). A. G. Lafley, for example, the estimable CEO of Proctor & Gamble, the world's largest consumer-products company, wields high expectations of his employees. When deficiencies do occur, the whip of accountability is not cracked if the nonperformers learn "early, fast, and cheap" from their mistakes. Leaders in any field, industry, or endeavor, Lafley insists, are not "lumps of clay" unsparingly molded by their plight. They do not create crises that do not exist, sort through the flattery, and see things as they are (Jones, 2007, p. 3B). As Jianlin (2004) states, "On the river east for 30 years, but the next 30 years will be on the river west." In the wake of reality we model honesty, integrity, and discipline in our "turnaround" decisions and actions.

Life is not perfect because we are not perfect, others are not perfect, and the world is not perfect! Non-acceptance of inevasible imperfection is like trying to "shovel away our shadows" (Reynolds,

1980, p. 105). There is little to gain but tension. Acceptance, on the other hand, frees us from restrictive uptightness and defensive impasse to become most actionable: going *with* and not *against* reality. As yoga students are taught: "To relax is not to collapse but simply to undo tension" (Scaravelli, 1991). Struggling ends when we stop struggling!

Concomitantly, the more powerful is our will (*sei no yokubo*) to live well the more we suffer in our faults and shortcomings. Suffering, therefore, is not what *arugamama* seeks to ameliorate but our dis-*position* toward suffering. The burden of unavoidable unhappiness is increased by unhappiness about being unhappy (Frankl, 1959, p. 180). To accept our imperfections is a rite of passage through where the river narrows and sputters. It is also preparation for *repositioning* ourselves to uphold the flow of life. *Arugamama* awakens us to our limits without being demoralized by them. The sizeable boulder in the riverbed may be un-moveable, but the river moves onward and leaves the boulder in its past.

Oversensitivity

Striving for perfection of health and character is a natural motivation within *sei no yokubo*. This is not the *over*perfectionism or "tyranny of the shoulds" of those who think that they should always succeed, like what they do, and be trouble free (Morita, 1928/1998). An overly idealistic and competitive mind-set wastes focus and energy for self-development. Moritists thus espouse:

> *Arugamama no jibun de ikiru.*

> Living as I am.
>
> (Hasegawa, 1993, p. 1)

This is not "benchmarking against the average." We may be *doing* our best without necessarily *being* the best. Cracks in a ceramic pot, for example, symbolize for the Japanese that nothing in art or life is impeccable. The artisan's skill is exemplified despite flaws in execution, because the Japanese decidedly prefer irregularity and incompleteness in art forms. The finest examples of the Bizen and Shigaraki styles are ceramics that are lopsided with bald patches of glaze and rough with tiny stones in the clay. As Kenkō wrote, "Leaving something incomplete makes it interesting and gives one the feeling that there is room for growth" (Keene, 1989, p. 131).

Among certain neurosis-prone individuals, however, there is found an acute oversensitivity to imperfections (*hipocondori seikicho* or "hypochondriacal temperament"). This type of individual exaggerates, rejects, or resists weaknesses in ability or personality, and, accordingly, is caught in a dilemma. There is no withdrawing from an active life (because of the high-powered drive to achieve) in order to avoid disclosure or reminder of the faults. At the same time, less satisfaction and greater risk are felt in social, romantic, or work situations because the prospect of failure is ruthlessly brought to mind.

The more we fixate on any imperfection, the more our awareness of it amplifies and prolongs. The more we are sensitive to it, the more we invest attention on it. The more we attend to it, the more the sensation grows — *ad infinitum*. Morita (Maeda & Nathan, 1999) termed this vicious cycle *seishin kogo sayo* ("psychic interaction"). Kora (1990) illustrates psychic interaction in patients suffering from headaches. The patients want emancipation from this symptom, because they believe that they can do anything if only they were free of it. Focusing on the headache, however, promotes its effect, which, in turn, exacerbates the headache. This psychic interaction will come to a halt if the patients consider it as something that has "possessed" them, and begin to believe that they must continue despite such a handicap (p. 10).

In this sequence of attention and sensation, attention is the more controllable. We cannot will to be insensitive but we can exercise control over the direction of our attention. We break the self-defeating obsession on imperfections by giving them *less* attention, thereby becoming less overpowered by them. The goal of Morita therapy is to restore *arugamama*, wherein "sensations are experienced in a flow" and the "actual living situation is accepted" (Maeda & Nathan, 1999, p. 528). We admit the quirks and quibbles of our lives and delve into what it takes to improve.

The small stuff

Daily living is mottled with the mildly inconvenient or slightly repulsive. Bumblers crassly cut into customer lines, loutishly yell on cellular phones, and absurdly blast horns in gridlock. These are momentary rubs that most of us readily accept as the *faux pas* of social commerce. When these occur, we infer the moment will pass and soon we will be further away from the irritant. "Don't fret a few Lilliputians now and then" is decent advice.

In an episode of the once-popular television series, *Candid Camera*, the contrived scene was a neighborhood bakery with a bogus handwritten sign on the counter: "We do not give change." Some customers, having the sign pointed out to them after having overpaid for their purchase, were infuriated and strongly protested. Other customers stood speechless and befuddled at the bakery's shocking new policy. Still others marched away peeved, shaking their heads in disbelief. But one gentleman unassumingly paid, took his baked goods, and turned to leave. Peter Funt, the show's host who was impersonating the shop proprietor, promptly summoned the man to return to the counter. Funt asked the customer why he hadn't questioned not receiving the change that was fairly due to him. The man politely answered: "I don't sweat anything. I don't let anyone rent space in my head."

The practice of *arugamama* does not mean that we do not let anyone or anything bother us. It does teach us to first identify what really is happening in order to act most responsibly. If we are a zebra being stalked by a lion on the Serengeti, we instantaneously know how to take action. Zebras don't get ulcers because they instinctively know to outrun a predator to survive (Sapolsky, 1998). Humans, however, become muddled in fantasies, denials, and half-truths. In order not to be "overrun and devoured" by even marginal stressors, we need to be accurate about what we face and practical about the concomitant course of action.

Sunao

Sunao is the Japanese word for "open" and "compliant." Its corollary, according to Fujita (1990), is maneuvering the daily stream of life with *kappatsu* ("spontaneity"). Blatner (2000) believes that this inclination relies on the elements of courageous engagement, willingness to take risks, and stretching of the mind. *Kappatsu* includes capable responses to new challenges and tonic recrudescence to old situations (Moreno, Blomkvist, & Rutzel, 2000).

We cannot, however, be pushed into being spontaneous; it must come from naturally attending to the "here-and-now."

The opposite of *sunao* is *shiso no mujun* ("conflict of thoughts" or "contradiction by ideas"), an attempt to contrive or manufacture a different reality than what exists: "If only I had . . ." "What if . . ." "It could have been different if . . ." *Shiso no mujun* is *un*reality, an "illusory subjective world" where fleeting thoughts are substituted for objective facts. As Morita (1975) explained, *shiso no mujun* misses the distinction between thought and reality. Thoughts are not reality. They are a description, explanation, or inference *about* reality.

The incongruity between what is (fact) and what we want it to be (ideal) can be galling. In reaction, we decry what is missing in life and either fall into falsehoods in order to align reality with our ideals or rack ourselves with self-pity, self-criticism, and self-indolence. Many of us, for example, have experienced the internal debate between alighting from a warm bed on a chilly morning and lingering under the covers. We know we must arise (ideal) to begin the day's work, but we procrastinate (fact). This inner conflict is the harbinger of neurosis. Attention is wrongly focused on yielding to or overcoming some momentary discomfort through an inner solution ("I'll wait until I feel like getting up"). Instead, attention must be directed toward *acting upon* those immediate tasks that "pull" us to complete them (arising from the bed).

The unacceptable

Michael J. Fox, the once boyish-looking film and television star, has Parkinson's, a presently incurable, degenerative neurological disorder that siphons away control over bodily movements: rigidity, tremors, lack of balance, and shuffling progress unabated. (Fox's young son lovingly calls him "Shaky Dad.") Fox (2002) concedes the havoc wrought by Parkinson's but is determined to be devoted to his wife and children, and to be a national advocate for fellow sufferers and stem cell research. Fox refuses to be ravaged by his declining health or emaciated career. He chooses to live, in Moritist terms, as a "functioning, acting, un-self-conscious being in motion that is always becoming" Kondo (1975, p. 255).

We must accept the absolutely unchangeable in order to change the absolutely unacceptable. The truth—at times dire, alarming, and shameful—must be absorbed despite the safeguards we have erected against disquieting self-evaluation. As Wagener (2003) describes, fantasy is a way to "soften" reality. We disguise the truth because it is sometimes very hard to take, especially the cold truth about our less appealing nature: our knotted anger, fears, and vulnerabilities. Temporarily, this one-dimensional strategy may suffice, but disaffecting from reality is a "precarious psychological space" as it edges us toward self-deception (p. 23). The sole arena where life must be met is the truthful and actual. To only rue over what is deficient, damaged, or lost is to miss enjoying the life we (still) do have. Realistic living may not yield commensurate results, but effort alone *is* happiness (*doryoku soku kofuku*).

Merging Currents: We know what is real through directly experiencing it.

Chapter 6

Morita Life Principle Six Experience

"Life flows from being intuitive"

Subjectivity or direct experiencing refers to the very experience of a sensation, a mood, a reaction, or a behavior. It is raw, intuitive awareness, free of critical thinking.

Shoma Morita
(1928/1974, p. 81)

Sho-ichi-nen

Morihei Ueshiba, the founder of aikido, never explained his techniques to students (cf. Frager, u.d.). A novice, according to Ueshiba, may be "intellectually conceited" about aikido but not at all technically proficient or committed to its life values. Ueshiba would thus *demonstrate* aikido's elliptical, soft movements as his students carefully watched. The students were then to experiment on one another, throw after throw, to "understand" the grace and power they had just observed. The students neither spoke to one another nor addressed Ueshiba. They discovered that this primary experiencing (*taiken*) is reliable because it derives from their own bodies in action.

Straightforward lessons in life reduce the misinterpretation of "easily misunderstood concepts" (Morita, 1928/1974, p. 81). Both in the martial arts and a personal lifeway, knowledge is reflected in bearing more than declaration. *Rikai* ("intellectual knowledge"), in contrast, is often abstract, judgmental, and less dependable. Morita (1928/1998) explained that his method of treatment does not expose clients to superficial, memory-oriented, or abstract knowledge. He believed that these methods are ineffective and even injurious. Passive therapy methods alone "reinforce idle, weak, fragile, and less than resistant characters." Treatment requires active methods to improve mental as well as physical health (p. 99).

Who thrives most in love? Is it the bystander glancing at the newborn being affectionately cradled or is it the doting mother herself? Who exults most from a breakthrough in cancer treatment? Is it the oncology intern who pores over a medical journal or the patient in remission? *Sho-ichi-nen* is the "original intention" or "genuine occurrence" of some sensation, mood, or behavior that casts little doubt as to what is gained, achieved, or learned, even if the mind does not fully comprehend. As Morita (1998) quipped, we only know the taste of food *after* we have eaten it. Those who have not tasted a certain food cannot savor it (or life) simply by words, no matter how vivid (p. 45).

The Japanese refer to this knowledge, based on immediate experience, as "gut enlightenment" or the way of *hara* (Yamaoka, 1976). The *hara* ("abdomen") is the source of calmness, stability, power, and flexibility. Both Hinduism and Buddhism teach that the *hara* is the natural focal point of physical, mental, and spiritual wellbeing through which vital energy flows. As a Zen master instructed a novice: "You must realize that the center of the universe is in the pit of your belly!" To be called *hara no hito* ("person of *hara*") is thus a noble compliment, indicating equilibrium of character and determination (Yamaoka, 1976, p. 4). This person is balanced, tranquil, warmhearted, magnanimous, and sympathetic, and intuitively responds to matters of life with *hara ga kirei* ("clean, beautiful *hara*"), not freakish and reckless behaviors.

Persuasive experience

Morita therapists do not overinstruct with thick advice, lengthy elucidation, or verbal confrontation to influence the views of their clients. The objective is not for clients to be able to articulate their troubles in a therapeutic setting. As Kennett (1972) warns, the "clear water of the mind" becomes ruffled by the winds of thought and reason (p. 16). Yamaoka (1976), moreover, explains that much of the tension that we experience daily arises out of our habits of thought. It is pointless for us to focus our attention to the mind in an attempt to free ourselves from this strain. This only leads to becoming more embroiled in the stress. The mind might be able to work out its problems in time, but "it cannot do so by itself alone" (p. 7).

Insight is obtained through uncluttering of our minds and foraying into personal discovery (cf. Kitanaka, 2003, p. 243). Levy (Reynolds & Yamamoto, 1972) inasmuch writes that clients who jump into life have a "greater therapeutic effect than dealing with verbal images in an office" (pp. 193-194). Morita (1928/1998) hence stated that the foundation of his therapy is to educate clients about nature and their lives, and once they experience the treatment, they trust it (pp. 34, 46). Morita called his approach "experiential therapy," "natural therapy," or "awakening therapy" (Kitanishi & Mori, 1995, p. 246). As Fujita (personal communication, October 20, 2004) enjoins, the "strongest power" is to refer clients to their own experiences:

> When you choose a book from the shelf to purchase, do you choose the one on the top? No, because the book is too soiled. This is the simple desire to live well . . . Patients do not know their own humanity. In work therapy patients forget their symptoms; they forget their efforts to forget their symptoms.

Kora (1990) adds that even if clients do not understand the nature of their symptoms or they entertain doubts as to the propriety of the treatment they are undergoing, their condition will still improve if they have followed the guidance and behaved as instructed. Once their condition starts to improve, they will then as well come to understand the nature of their symptoms (p. 8). The goal of Morita therapy is therein not for clients to receive persuasive counsel but to incorporate persuasive experiences, which is the more creditable point of intervention (LeVine, 1993). These experiences are those of *familiar* responsibilities, not tasks fabricated to keep clients busy or undertaken to hasten recovery. Many years ago, Kora (1968) reminds, a woman came to Carlisle complaining of the vicissitudes in human relationships. He told her to begin by putting her sewing box in order (p. 324).

Light switch insight

A 35-year-old female client, "Rebecca," living in her parents' home, reported that she had a long-suffering relationship with her mother, usually detonated with disparaging snipes. Teaching Rebecca basic principles of interpersonal communication might have seemed warranted, but greater promise was found winnowing out a recent occurrence of trouble and creating a solution. An area of repeated contention was the failure of Rebecca to shut off her bedroom light when she left for work in the morning. Her mother would belittle her for not being able to carry out such a rudimentary act. Rebecca's retort had been several-fold:

- Her mother should shut off the light without grumble just as she does for her mother when she forgets to do so with the bathroom light.
- When she wakes in the morning, it is still dark. By the time she departs for work, it is daylight so she does not always notice the light being on.
- Her father ineptly installed the light switch upside down so it is confusing if the light is on or off by just glancing at the switch as she exits the room.
- She has repeatedly asked her father to fix the light switch, but he always replies that he is too busy working on his motorcycles.

Rebecca viewed her life as populated with "traitorous gremlins." She deflected all blame to her mother, the sunlight, the light switch, and her father — to everywhere and everyone else!

Our responsibility is not the behavior of others but our own. The mother *could* have been less faultfinding and her father more obliging. The reality is they were not. Although it would seem that the fuss about the light switch was petty amongst broader family issues, the Moritist aims to address life *in detail* and then extend these lessons to other areas. Rebecca was thus guided to concentrate on resolving the problem of the light switch. She decided to affix a written reminder adjacent to the switch. Over several days, she experimented with the note's size, color, and shape. This did help but the reversed position of the switch still periodically "caused" Rebecca not to shut off the light. Since she could not afford an electrician, I asked Rebecca if she had ever installed a light switch herself. Her sarcastic reply was that since she had such an imbroglio just shutting off the switch, what made me think she might ever have dared to replace one!

One approach could have been to try to inculcate enough confidence in Rebecca for her to attempt the task. I could then have referred her to the public library to read about the installation of a light switch, or have her call an electrician for step-by-step instructions. I instead escorted Rebecca to the fuse box in my office, demonstrated how to shut off the electrical power, and then walked with her to one of the light switches. I removed the first screw of the coverplate and then placed the screwdriver in Rebecca's hand. She finished unscrewing the plate. I then unfastened the first screw of the inside switch itself, and Rebecca unscrewed the second one. She then reversed the switch and reinstalled it and the plate. After Rebecca turned back on the electrical power and tested the switch, we reviewed what she done. Now more confident *after* accomplishing this task, she went home and immediately corrected her bedroom switch. Thereafter, Rebecca infrequently forgot to shut off the light, and appraised herself as more resilient, resourceful, and competent (cf. Charlesworth & Jackson, 2004).

Rebecca's mother was so impressed with her daughter's initiative that she shed most of her abrasive criticisms. Overall family communication was improved. The mother, appreciating Rebecca's new display of reliance, broached the topic of mounting household expenses, including electricity costs. Rather than feeling threatened by disapproval, Rebecca sought a joint solution with her mother. She soon agreed to pay a manageable portion of the monthly bills. For Rebecca, one "instance of success" (cf. Miller, Hubble, & Duncan, 1996) was the kiln for other responsible actions and the quelling of her family's turmoil.

Experiencing truth
Karen Horney (1885-1952), the iconic New York psychiatrist, briefly studied Morita Therapy in Japan before her untimely death

(LeVine, 1994). Horney, influenced by Morita's therapeutic methods, described life "not as a problem to be solved but an experience to be realized" (Horney, 1952, p. 4). The fundamental task is not so much to acquire a philosophical view of the world but to develop an intimate relation with it through our experiences. As Zenists hold (Ives, 1992, p. 71), practice without study is blind ("has no eyes"), but study without practice is powerless ("has no legs"). There must be *gakugyō-ichinyo* ("unity of study and practice").

Beliefs are formed, according to Morita (1998, p. 7), as we transfer experiential knowledge into actions that become expressions of our character. D. T. Suzuki (1991) concurs that personal experience is everything in Zen. The foundation of all concepts is unsophisticated experience; it is around this that Zen constructs all the scaffolding known as *goruku* ("sayings"). Though the scaffolding affords a useful means to reach the utmost reality, it is still an elaboration and artificiality (pp. 33-34).

Words are fastened to experiences, but replicating our experience of truth is more important than explicating dogma (cf. Ogawa, 1972). Language tends to pull us away from experience by giving the impression of permanence. Life itself is peripatetic. The explanation of how best to live must, therefore, continuously seek to accommodate *all* the experiences we encounter and *any* possible others. As Thich Nhat Han (u.d.), a Vietnamese Zen master, affirms:

> Our true home is in the present moment. To live in the present moment is a miracle. The miracle is not to walk on water. The miracle is to walk on the green Earth in the present moment, to appreciate the peace and beauty that are available now. Peace is all around us-in the world and in nature-and within us-in our bodies and in our spirits. Once we learn to touch this peace, we will be healed and transformed. It is not a matter of faith; it is a matter of practice.

Truth, in this way, is *egalitarian*: it is attainable by more than ascetics, geniuses, and saints. Merit (*jiriki*) is achieved and grace (*tariki*) is found in the itinerary of living. Once we have heard this "melody" of life, we will not ever again doubt it (cf. Smullyan, 1977, p. 19).

Kofu

Meditation is an exceptional though not exclusive pathway to intuitive experience. It is paying attention in a particular way. There are four "instruments" of meditative attention: the body, intellect, emotions, and action (Sheikh & Sheikh, 1989, p. 438). These are manifested in various ways, including, respectively, Hassidic dancing, Zen mindfulness, "awakened heart," and "benevolent presence." Paying attention, in other words, is more than just seeing with our eyes, because even with our eyes closed we can increase awareness and settle into a state for receiving. The aim of meditation is not necessarily greater effectiveness in the everyday world but transcending ordinary confusion (Kirmayer, 2002, p. 310). It is therefore practiced by some while enveloped in settings of solitude and serenity. As Tollifson (1999) witnesses, meditation is communing with the "silent clouds blowing by" and a solitary orange that plops from the tree, landing in wet black earth and glistening leaves (pp. 99-100). Meditation creates this sense of peace not from attaining something absent but from *un*doing through centering of the mind and body.

Some forms of meditation may appear uncomfortable or severe. Sitting cross-legged in a full lotus position, modulating breathing, and not clinging or submitting to intrusive thoughts might appear trance-like and stoic. The discipline of *zazen*, for example, is the preferred daily practice of Zen followers who seek to still the "monkey mind" of internal chaos and find the "deep truths of Zen" first intelligible in the innermost soul (cf. Suzuki, 1991). Long hours of *zazen*, often in the midst of emotional and physical pain, cultivate a high degree of self-discipline and perseverance. Practitioners discover inner strength that makes it possible to function with greater wisdom, creativity, and effectiveness in the face of adversity. Ives (1992) writes that this "deepened composure" develops the steadiness for sustained, committed action (p. 37).

Hypnosis is also highly focused attention that enhances our control over body sensation and function as well as alters how we perceive and process reality. Its clinical application for depression, post-traumatic stress disorder, substance abuse, pain management, and other problems have been well documented (Chapman, 2006; Dowd & Healey, 1986). Being mindful — exercising our consciousness of the here and now — is, however, neither a mystical haven reserved for shaven heads and saffron robes nor a therapist-coaxed state for those whose personality trait registers hypnotizability. The particular way of meditation takes intent and cultivation, but is not an exceptional talent. All of us are able to and should meditate (Kabat-Zinn, 1994), even if this is apportioned to "meaningful pauses" in the day or the "mobile meditation" in which bicyclers and trekkers revel. We can enter *any* experience meditatively to become more fully in touch with life.

In yoga the body becomes the meditative vehicle. This is similar to what Morita and Zen call *kofu*, the naturalness in bodily action when the mind allows the body the full harmony of its own coordination (LeVine, 2004). As Parker (1998) writes, through attending to corporal sensation, weight, gravity, posture, and pliability, we honor often disregarded parts of the body. The detailed instruction in yoga poses (e.g., "Focus attention on the four corners of your hand" or "Turn your left foot out 45 degrees") trains us to intrinsically and fully inhabit our bodies. In doing so, we learn to fully inhabit our worlds (Parker, 1998, p. 1).

Equally, when we direct our awareness to unnoticed or neglected areas of our lives, we enjoy a more complete and lucid existence. It does not matter if we are chanting mantras or doing housework. Only the *quality* of the experience matters. In life, we are not so much *over*whelmed by a deluge of events as *under*whelmed in our connection to what we are experiencing. As Needleman (Hammond and Ferguson, 1998) echoes, we live in this "little dark basement of this huge palace" that is the center of perception and energy. When the body, mind, and feeling are together, we are close to being a "receptacle for something very great" (p. 79).

Nichijo seikatsu

Life is not experienced in cryptic generalities. When we therefore amalgamate distinctions into catchphrases, we debauch what we are immediately and objectively experiencing. Ishiyama (2004) points to the following:

- Overgeneralization of a life condition
  ("I'm always . . ." or "I get totally whenever . . .");
- Self-exceptionalism
  ("I am a special case"); and

- Pessimistic self-assessment
  ("I'm always so nervous" or "I'm a helpless one").

At an international Morita training in Japan in the mid-1980s, one of the participants was an American psychiatrist. He blithely announced that he was eager to sit endless hours listening to the lectures and parsing the content of the readings. We advised him and the other students that the pivotal lessons would come from daily life (*nichijo seikatsu*) rather than "over-intellectualizing." Though displeased, the psychiatrist nodded his accord. We then explained that there are different footwear for distinct areas of the training residences and grounds. This custom was not only for functionality and cleanliness but also to show respect for others. There were durable *geta* ("wooden clogs") for the outdoors, soft indoor tabbies that would not scrape the *tatami* ("straw flooring"), and impermeable slippers for the separately housed toilet. Since we would all share the assortment of footwear, it was important that we follow specific courtesies:

- correct footwear be worn and returned to their proper location;
- footwear were to be neatly replaced to make it most convenient for the next user to slip into; and
- footwear should be placed so as not to obstruct the walkway.

The psychiatrist impatiently took note.

Several of us slept in a room with individual Japanese bedrolls (*futon*). In the middle of the night, we were awakened by the commotion of the psychiatrist bounding toward the outside toilet. We could hear the toilet door open and slam. Minutes later we heard the toilet door again, and then the psychiatrist galloping to his bed. The next morning we awoke and saw the psychiatrist asleep with the foul *toilet* slippers lying within inches of his face! He had trampled through the house only drowsily attentive. He might come to intellectually understand the Morita principles of *alertness* and *thoughtfulness*, but would he actually live them with insight gleaned from his everyday actions?

Sensei

The conundrum of how much genetic predisposition ("nature") and environmental influences ("nurture") interact to form who we are has been the centerpiece of human development theories (cf. Belsky, 2007). In this regard, Moritists interpret intrinsic life energy (*sei no yokubo*) and life experience (*taitoku*) working together in an unbroken ring of cause and effect. Innate tendencies materialize through deliberate practice. In Japanese tradition such practice falls under the guidance of a *sensei* ("teacher"). The *sensei* directs proper daily conduct leading to personal growth, compressing the student's self-inflated pride whenever correction is needed (Ishiyama, 1988, pp. 254-256).

> A Zen Master was asked by his student, "What is the Tao?" He replied, "I will tell you after you have drunk up the waters of the West River in one gulp."
> The student countered, "I have already drunk up the waters of the West River in one gulp."
> To which the Master replied, "Then I have already answered your question."
>
> (Smullyan, 1977, p. 4)

The *sensei* offers advisement, sometimes stern and sometimes dispassionate, because it is the student's responsibility to develop skill at living rather than simply imitate the *sensei*. Learning does not originate in the student nor does it end with the teacher. As the Buddhist tale goes, a young man seeking erudition, sat motionless at the foot of the Zen master. The master handed the presumptuous pupil a rake with the curt instruction to sweep the twigs and leaves from the pathway. Puzzled, the young man restated his request to be enlightened through the master's *words* of wisdom. Again, the master pointed to the awaiting pathway. The young man hesitated in order to protest but, seeing the steadfastness of the master, reluctantly decided to turn to his assignment.

At first, the student grumbled to himself about the time he was wasting. He would often peek toward the master in the distance to decipher his approval. The master was not even paying attention to him! The young man eventually decided to assiduously launch into his task to quickly finish it and return to his quest. As he more and more focused on raking thoroughly, his arms began swaying more efficiently. His eyes also began more rapidly detecting how each piece of fallen debris moved with the nuances of the breeze. More and more the young man learned to economize his movements. After a time, he no longer was mindful of his discontent and immersed himself in *just raking*. As his mind and body arrived at wholly acting as one, he experienced the wisdom he was seeking!

Morita therapists likewise focus their clients on the "here and now" of the didactic interaction or concrete lesson before them. This may include the use of role-play, imagery, and metaphors (Ishiyama, 2004). The client observes certitude rather than accepts hearsay. In effect, the therapist-client relationship recedes and becomes "hidden" when clients let go of resistance and jump into doing (Kitanishi & Mori, 1995, p. 251). The Japanese term for this is *te narai* ("hands-on learning") or rigorous discipline in the pursuit of excellence.

The *sensei*, accordingly, models rather than recites the dead text so there is a "living current" to truth. The trustworthiness of Morita therapists lies in their personal character and practical skills, life experience and abilities. No teacher should insist that we swallow whole a set of principles without verification through our own discipline. D. T. Suzuki (1991) writes that Zen strongly and persistently insists on inner spiritual experience. The sacred sutras and their exegesis by the wise and learned are "not of intrinsic importance" (p. 33).

Our innate life energy feeds the search for meaning in life. At times this may be just seeking a way out of unbearable circumstances or the trap we feel life has become. There must be a better way to live than what we have made it to be thus far! Morita (1928/1998), however, noted that the more we attempt to pursue comfort and pleasure, the more we fall into a state of disappointment and pessimism until we believe our desires will remain unfulfilled (p. 83). Instinctive yearning requires guidance from those wiser or more experienced. We may accept them as teachers or not, but, as has been said, if you come face to face with the Buddha on the road, one of you is going in the wrong direction!

The word *sensei* is literally "one who comes before," whether a shaman on journey or devoted fellow pilgrim. In the *Seikatsu-no*

Hakkenkai (Discovery of Life Association), therefore, lay group members provide mutual support through *sokatsu*, summaries of personal struggles (Hasegawa, 1990). Senior members (some of whom are only coincidentally certified by the Japan Morita Society) guide junior members (H. Yokoyama, personal communication, October 22, 2004), who are humbled in that someday they will in turn teach others.

Years ago, at a presentation on Morita therapy before a group of American psychologists, I inquired how many integrated into their own lives the principles they were teaching their clients. After a long, awkward pause, only one of the thirty psychologists present raised his hand, and another half-lifted her hand. The consensus was that the principles they promoted were applicable to "mental illness" or "behavioral dysfunction" and, hence, not intended for those (specifically themselves) not afflicted. The same question posed to a gathering of Morita therapists would produce a chorus of hands.

As Kondo (LeVine, 2004) writes: "Therapeutic moments occur when a patient absorbs the healthy part of the therapist. The therapist must therefore enter with a pure mind." The *sensei*, that is, relates to the student out of empathy, self-esteem, and integrity and not from egotistical detachment and dry authority. It is neither the Rogerian-style non-directive support of a client's self-actualization (Kitanaka, 2003) nor the absoluteness of "Do as I say" or "Do as I say I do." It is the invitation of "Do as I also do." Intersecting experience brings about mutual obligation, loyalty, and trust. We *all* can learn to live better each and every day.

Merging Currents: In the genuine experience of life we find renewal and rebirth.

Chapter 7

Morita Life Principle Seven
Mercy

"Life flows from being *for*-giving"

Deception occurs when we do not face the four inevitable events in human life (suffering, aging, becoming ill, and dying); whereas, true faith represents the transcendence of ego.

Shoma Morita
(1928/1998, p. 96)

Natural renewal

Life at the aerial, terra firma, and subterranean levels is always in some phase of regeneration. This natural rebirth guarantees that the world's energy remains complete (cf. Albom, 1997, p. 141). African elephants, for example, often uproot trees on the savannah in order to reach the highest leaves. Tourists on safari watch aghast at the seeming wanton devastation of scattered grassland trees. They decree that the marauding elephants must be stopped. Herd the elephants to an outlying area! Erect steel barricades! Unwittingly, the outraged tourists are overmagnifying a single thread of a life-sustaining garment. The elephants, in fact, are *contributing* to the preservation of the complex ecosystem. Since the leaves that the elephants consume can only be partially digested, the excreted fibrous dung is carried away as foodstuff by foraging insects. The toppled trees provide more easily attained nourishment for other animals. Plant life flourish from the sunlight penetrating through the less dense vegetation. The decomposing branches add to the soil's fertility. Dying and decay provide nutrients and prospect for reemergence and budding.

Taoism affirms that "peace exists in the center of continual destruction and construction," because the rule of natural law is to replenish, restore, and repeat (Loy, 1985, p. 78). This truism is luminous in my home state of Hawaii. On the Big Island, the Kilauea ("much spreading") caldera—home to Pele, the temperamental fire goddess—has spewed molten lava along its east rift zone since January 3, 1983. It is arguably the most active volcano in the world. Its first eruption occurred 300,000-600,000 years before present, and it has erupted 34 times since 1952 (United States Geological Survey [USGS], 2006). Kilauea's river of magma begins at the cinder-and-spatter cone of Pu'u 'O'o, and slices through the earth in a network of tubes, surfacing to leave smoldering property, burnt groves, and cannibalized lives in its wake. The fiery magma finally tumbles at 2,200 Fahrenheit into cool ocean waters, emitting billows of steam. A black delta forms of unstable lava, rock, and sand until it solidifies into a pavinglike surface and forms new land. The lava's tumultuous path concludes with a kind of apology.

The loop of mercy is also propelled by earth's grand hydrologic system. Evaporation sets in motion precipitation, and watersheds pour into catch basins and reservoirs to keep our planet nourished and lush. Old waters rework into new rivers. The oceans, moreover, are never still themselves. Their tides and currents move massive amounts of water around the world, and have a great influence on the water cycle. The Kuroshio Current, off the shores of Japan, is the largest of these "rivers." It can travel between 25 and 75 miles per day, 1-3 miles per hour, and extends some 3,300 feet deep. The Gulf Stream sends warm water from Mexico across the Atlantic Ocean towards Great Britain at a speed of 60 miles per day. This stream moves 100 times as much water as all terrestrial rivers on earth (USGS, 2005).

Destabilization of the earth's water rotation comes primarily from human recklessness: greenhouse gas emissions and global warming; deforestation and erosion; and degradation of wetlands and depletion of water storage areas (Sophocleous, 2004). Mountain glacier and snow cover are shrinking in most of the world, resulting in decreased spring and summer flow volumes in rivers, and increased winter flows. Water is a finite—there is no appreciable water entering or leaving the earth from space—but renewable resource (Wood, 2003). Since the world's easily captured water is already identified and allocated, humans must improve efficiency, alter allocations, and develop new sources. Fortunately, we are able to reverse deficient practices and advance scientific remediation. We must translate what it means to be beneficiaries of the forces of natural renewal to becoming its agents.

As Morita (1928/1998, p. 89) stated, a person may well call upon Buddha, God, or the Absolute, but pragmatic faith rests in the truth made obvious through natural events. We thrive not only because of human enterprise but also because of a magnanimous universe. Palingenesis, for example, safeguards individual human life. The human body is porous to disease and susceptible to injury but also primed to heal. Our uncompromised immune system wards off viral invasions, homeoplasia forms new tissue, and broken bones fuse together. In much of Western medicine, we have yet to fully partner with this *vis medicatrix naturae* ("healing power of natural life processes").

About the time Morita was introducing his therapy, McNutt (1923), speaking to the San Francisco Medical Society, repeated the Hippocratic dictum, "Nature is the physician of disease." There is, McNutt reminded, an inherent power of recovery in the body that works from a "law which obtains throughout all nature" (p. 511). Mercifulness is embedded in life. This determinism secures individual freedom and obliges personal responsibility for human wellbeing (Loy, 1985, p. 84).

Second chance

On December 30, 1903, 600 patrons—many women and children—perished when a fire broke out in Chicago's Iroquois

Theater. The theater had been open less than a month and was supposedly fireproof. It was standing room only for a holiday matinee of a popular musical. The theater management, however, had not followed well developed fire precautions, including the proper installation of an emergency asbestos screen that would descend rapidly to separate the audience from burning scenery. In order to keep out gatecrashers, the management had also added locked gates over exit doors, while other doors—similar to those in private residences—opened *inwards*. An accidental fire erupted when a hot light ignited a velvet curtain, and spread rapidly through the crowded theater. Terrorized patrons rushed through the engulfing flames and toxic smoke toward the exits, only to discover them locked or not opening outward as needed! The panic-stricken throng piled wave after wave against the doors, trampling to death many of the theatergoers. Bodies were amassed ten feet high in some exits (O'Brien & Benedict, 2004).

The horrific death toll generated the review of fire safety in public buildings nationwide, including doorway designs. Doors were subsequently installed to swing *outward* and equipped with panic devices. A metal release was mounted across the inside width of each door. Pressing against the bar at any point disengages the door lock to permit swift and easy exit. This invention has become so familiar that today we do not even realize its origin in tragedy or its facility for saving lives. If this safety enhancement had not been made, the Iroquois Theater would only be remembered as the venue of a lethal and culpable malfeasance.

Every exit (from peril) is simultaneously an entrance (to safety). Every departure from a detrimental way of life is a threshold to a second chance, even if it is not always "plainly seen and immediately heard" (Banks 1983). As Millman (1992) writes, difficult persons and situations are among the "surest doorways" to improve our lives, because they "get our attention and reveal our weak areas" (p. 25). Even our most troubling personal failings—the things we should have done and did not do—can be rectified. What we mete out or fall victim to transposes into the opportunity (*kikai*) for redemption. This may be pain-inducing, but it is the way to "clear old karmas." Giving birth induces labor pains, especially when we are the one being reborn (Millman, 1996, p. 37).

For-giveness and forgetting

Forgiveness is an act of utmost mercy in that there is no recompense demanded and no claim of entitlement. Forgiveness must be unconditionally ministered *and* meekly accepted for the circle of healing to occur. South African President Nelson Mandela spent numerous years imprisoned for his political and humanness beliefs. The first 18 years were spent on Robben Island, working in a rock quarry and living in a cramped cell. Mandela flatly refused, however, to levy vengeance on the white establishment that riled against him for his heroic anti-apartheid stance. As Bill Clinton (2004) records in his presidential memoir:

> I said, "Mandiba" — Mandela's colloquial tribal name, which he asked me to use — "I know you did a great thing in inviting your jailers to your inauguration, but didn't you really hate those who imprisoned you?"
>
> He replied, "Of course I did, for many years. They took the best years of my life. They abused me physically and mentally. I didn't get to see my children grow up . . . Then one day when I was working in the quarry, hammering the rocks, I realized that they had already taken everything from me except my mind and my heart. Those they cannot take without my permission. I decided not to give them away."
>
> I asked him another question. "When you were walking out of prison for the last time, didn't you feel the hatred rise up in you again?"
>
> "Yes," he said, "for a moment I did. Then I thought to myself, 'They have had me for 27 years. If I keep hating them, they will still have me.' I wanted to be free, and so I let it go."
>
> (AARP, 2004, p. 72)

Nonviolence rather than bloody strife was Mandela's weaponry. His single-minded purpose was to remove the yoke of racism and not dispatch revenge. As Mandela knew, withholding of forgiveness sinks us into the dangerous swamp of the murky past where the alligators of animosity swarm and bite! Unrelenting resentments and longstanding grudges harden temperament. The more we protract hostility, the more we become that acrimony. We then track every slight, nurse all humiliation, and belabor each hurt into our personality and way of life. *Feeling* unforgiving is natural, but *remaining* unforgiving is poisonous. Confucius taught, "If you devote your life to seeking revenge, first dig two graves."

Morita (1928/1998) differentiated between "forgiveness" and "forgetting." Forgiveness is an act and forgetting is knowledge. We can purposely forgive but we cannot deliberately forget. We will remember when and how we forgive, but when and how we forget is like not knowing when and how we fall asleep. We therefore have responsibility to forgive but no responsibility to forget (p. 13). In fact, *not* being able to forget may kindle the power to give our lives to something worthwhile. Freddie Mae Baxter, a 75-year-old African American storyteller, grew up in a South Carolina shack without electricity, hot water, or a father. Her mother raised eight children through hardscrabble times. Baxter, dropping out of middle school, moved north and worked in New Jersey as a housekeeper and nanny. A generous heart and her share of fun ("I'm no stone," she says) keep her from bitterness toward the sociopolitical hierarchy that relegates some to the cellar. "People need to do some forgiving," she preaches. "Just go ahead and live life today" (Carlin & Fowler, 1999, p. 80).

Least harmful

In the Japanese martial art of aikido a belligerent adversary is vanquished not with ferocious counter strikes and mortal force. Violence is met with deflection, a harmonizing of the aggressor's *ki* ("energy") with our own to yield the *least* violent result. The aim is not brutish strength to annihilate the opponent. It's about how *little* harm we can inflict and still exercise control of the situation. Correspondingly, we do not become casualties of the enmity of others if we mark a more aspirational course for our lives. We respond to ill-will not by contesting its full might but by redirecting its intensity.

Forgiveness is therefore not a psychological "switch" in mindset as it is action *for* giving. It is turning attention *away from* what others have wrongfully done to us toward what we now rightfully *give our lives to* in spite of (or because of) what has happened. For-giveness is an ethical and productive parry to maltreatment by others. As long as we wallow in loathing, we are handcuffed to a past dominated by the offending person. When we continue to blame someone else for our lack of wellbeing, we remain the victim: vulnerable and small. At some point, letting go of grievances frees us to live: bold and large. As the satirical newspaper cartoon depicts, an inmate vacuously stares through the prison bars he clenches. The gloom in his eyes reflects hopelessness and helplessness. The irony is that he is too preoccupied with his predicament to notice that there are no actual sides to his cell! He needs only to release his hold and step around to freedom.

The promise of mercy, furthermore, never dries up as we re-channel its overflow into the lives of others. It is truly then that our lives can be *for* giving. As Holocaust survivor and therapist Viktor Frankl (1955) verifies, meaning in life comes from helping others find meaning in life. This, nonetheless, may or not involve reconciliation. Reconciliation, for example, is hardly the prescription for abused spouses whose domineering partners continue the beatings while intermittently proclaiming remorse and begging forgiveness. For-giveness is not part of a marriage covenant to serially submit to destructive coupling. For-giveness in chronically abusive relationships is accepting that the battering may likely continue, separating safely from the relationship, and not being manacled by the illusion of the abuser's reform (cf. Ogawa, 1997).

Abusers exert control to remain the *center of attention*. Persons who suffer abuse assume control over their lives by attending increasingly and responsibly to their own wellbeing. The biblical admonition to "love your enemies" does not mean to reside or sleep with abusers, or clean and cook for them! It may entail cautious support for *their* welfare, including the constructive prospects afforded by separation/incarceration and therapy/reeducation. We do not have to forgo justice or condone rotten behavior to for-give. Curiously, our wellbeing is not totally antithetical to the wellbeing of the transgressor. In some ways for-giveness is selfish because it reduces the stress of staying in a state of unforgiveness. It takes a ponderous load of emotional, spiritual, and physical energy to brood.

Ground zero

The Chinese sometimes render the salutation "May you live in interesting times!" The times that unduly pressure us at the core of our security and beliefs, however, can make us wish for the humdrum. As Wheeler (1999) chronicles, when chaos shakes the very ground under our feet or the cries of the world are heard, we "must protest until we encounter mercy" (pp. 14-15). If this mercy is a false premise, the swelling tonnage of evil would have crushed humanity long ago. We could not live on if there was no abatement.

No American citizen will ever forget the morning of September 11, 2001. The images of the terrorist assaults, particularly on New York's World Trade Center, still torment us: the hijacked airliners' paths to target and explosion; billowing smoke and inferno; astonishing disintegration of towering steel and concrete into rubble; and distraught faces of family members searching for their missing loved ones. The grim task of digging out the remains of the deceased at Ground Zero lasted for more than eight months. Gallant recovery teams worked day in and day out under glaring lights and noise of heavy machinery to sift through 1.8 million tons of wreckage. Seething rage and anguish were mixed with unbridled teamwork and grit. Lt. Bill Keegan of the Port Authority Police gives testimony that just as the mountain of destruction is removed, the mountain of anger must at some point clear in order for us to architect goodness rather than erect hate (Sheehy, 2002, p. 6).

Anger and hate do grow fainter over time. The impermanence of what we presently feel saves us even as the tragic events they connect to may be long remembered. Kora (1968, p. 322) writes that regardless how high and pounding the waves of (any) emotions may be, they will recede and dwindle in time. If they were interminably draconian as the inceptive blow, none of us would have the heart to continue living.

Merging Currents: The harmonizing and liberating qualities of mercy are authenticated by how emotions complement one another.

Chapter 8

Morita Life Principle Eight
Feelings

"Life flows from being emotion-all"

Joy is just joy and sorrow is just sorrow.
Shoma Morita
(1928/1998, p. 88)

Thin emotions

The fantastically varied climes and ecosystems of Japan's 3,900 islands entertain tropical coral reefs to frigid ice-capped mountains. Even among Japan's four major islands there is remarkable variation from northern Hokkaido to southern Kyushu, and the Pacific Ocean on the east to Japan Sea on the west. There are four pronounced seasons with summers of sweltering humidity and winters of deep layers of snow. Having lived in Kansas for a number of years, however, I can attest that this state's weather is at least as formidable and volatile. The hottest day recorded in Kansas was 121° F on July 24, 1936, and the coldest−40° F on February 13, 1905. Kansas is also centrally located within our nation's "tornado alley," and annually has the most severe twisters (F5 on the Fujita Scale of wind damage). This "concentrated violence" (Williams, 1997) and the wide-open spaces of a pancake, featureless terrain, produce what Kansas residents refer to as "wild, plentiful air" (Heath-Moon, 2001). Booming thunderstorms, crackling lightening, and rowdy prairie winds are standard to life in the American Heartland!

According to a Chinese proverb, human emotions are even more tenuous than capricious weather: "Spring ice is thin but human emotions are more thin" (Char, 1970, p. 27). Emotions regularly match prevailing circumstances: downheartedness during an employment slump and joy while wading in effusive praise. Emotions may also be enigmatic: downheartedness at an employee's gala and joy while pulverized with scandalous tirades. Emotional states are not solely instigated through human exchange (Lock, 1993). They may or may not coincide with what we hope to feel at any given moment.

The Persian poet, Rumi (1207-1273), advises that being human is a "guesthouse." Every morning there is a new arrival or unexpected visitor: a joy, depression, or meanness. Even if a "crowd of sorrows" savagely sweeps our house and empties it of furniture, we are to treat each guest honorably. Although we would rather welcome and lodge certain emotions (e.g., elation or solace), and shun and evict others (e.g., glumness or irritation), our emotions elude our rule as the weather evades our command. One of the features of emotions is that they cannot be directly manipulated or managed at will (Morita, 1928/1998, p. 13). All exhortations of "Don't worry," "Be happy," or "Don't be sad" imply that what we feel is what we *choose* to feel. This is both illusory and flawed. We can no more fabricate non-stop euphoria than christen forth a balmy summer while freeze-dried in a blizzard!

Waves

Suppose that you pledged to be only cheery and carefree on a given day. You awaken with a shimmering smile and light-heartedly bounce out of bed into a bubbly douse in the shower. You dress in dazzling colors, leap into your gleaming convertible, and drive unimpeded down the expressway, performing fabulous *karaoke* to the radio with your car purring like a tiger. Happy! Happy! Happy! Suddenly, the traffic begins to slow, but it doesn't matter. Traffic snarls are no match for your blithesome glide. Nothing, you assure yourself, will dim the glow of the day.

As you peer ahead you begin to see the signs of a crash. You are startled by the sight of a maimed child on the roadway. A man is staggering nearby. Rage starts to fester within you seeing that a drunk driver apparently caused the death of an innocent life. What happened to your unassailability? Can you, should you, ignore the grisliness of the scene? Morita (1928/1998), referencing a Zen saying, writes that if we try to eliminate a wave with another wave, we will invite numerous waves (p. 39). We must learn to face the waves of emotions and "ride" them whenever and however they come. At times, we naturally feel "upbeat" and, at other times, downright "beat-up." Kora (1968) therefore writes that depending upon the importance of the event, its special characteristics, and the personality of the individuals, the ups and downs of the waves of emotions will diminish and disappear when left alone, *whether we like it or not* (p. 322).

Flexors and extensors

The emerging discipline of affective neuroscience studies individual differences in emotional reactivity and mood regulation related to brain structures and functioning (Davidson, 2003). Studying the "central circuitry of emotion," it seeks to identify influences on the "plasticity" of individual affective styles: why and how humans respond differently to the common stimuli to which we are exposed. Ostensibly, there are two poles of emotional states: one continuum is from "pleasant" to "unpleasant," and the other "activation" (arousal) to "deactivation" (sleep). We are said to either emotionally approach or withdraw from an event depending if it meets or threatens our basic needs (Davidson, 2000). A high activation to an unpleasant event, for example, might elicit a tense or nervous response while a pleasant event brings about an alert or excited one (Kaufman, 1999).

Affective neuroscience (Gross, 2002), moreover, describes two major strategies to regulate emotions so that we do not over-react (which might provoke adverse social consequences such as embarrassment or judgment): *reappraisal* (changing the way a situation is construed) and *suppression* (inhibiting the outward signs of inner feelings). By decreasing the subjective intensity of an experience, we can allegedly control responding "too emotionally." Emotions are adjudged to be "primitive" without the intervention of cognition (Davidson, 2000). We are not meant to live with just cold cognition — we are warm emotional beings — but we also cannot survive without the interaction and overlap of thinking and feeling.

The work of affective neuroscience helps us to understand the bio-psychological aspects of our emotions. Moritists, nonetheless, do not regard the attempt to modulate feelings as a realistic control point in our lives. Accepting feelings *as they are* and directing our attention to necessary action is more practical and rewarding. This is not the abandonment of a sense of control but rather *well-placed effort*. The presetting of emotions into positive and negative castes by affective neuroscientists also seems unnatural and unnecessary to Moritists, because emotions are naturally *compatible* and *symbiotic*.

When death stings us, for example, with the loss of a love one, would we want to hold that person less dear in order to grieve less? We grieve because we love. Living brings unpleasantness. Trying to get rid of unpleasantness sidetracks our original desire to live fully (Fujita, 2004). Kondo (1975) writes that in the reality of life, just as flexors and extensors complement each other in effecting smooth muscle movement, seemingly contradictory feelings help the stream of life flow in a balanced, harmonious way, if no artificial, intellectual intervention by the "either-or" principle is introduced (p. 255).

In other words, there is no "good" or "bad" affixed to what we feel at any given time. We have the freedom (perhaps obligation) to experience *any* feeling and *every* emotion (cf. Albom, 1997, pp. 103-105). Being emotion-*all* means accepting *whatever* emotions we experience. The hipster, "Go with how you are feeling!" is more ethically, "Feel how you are going!" Morita (1928/1998, p. 100) thus counseled his clients to authentically and fully experience the unprompted nature and variety of their feelings. Emotional health is the capacity to feel emotions genuinely ("Don't let go too soon."), and then acquiesce to their natural elapse ("Don't hold on too long."). Albom (1997) reiterates that by throwing ourselves into emotions, by allowing ourselves to dive in, all the way, over our heads even, we expressly experience them. We then know what pain is. We then know what love is. We then know what grief is. And only then can we say that we have recognized and experienced that emotion (p. 104).

This latitude toward emotions enables us to more fully engage life in all its twists and turns, highs and lows. All emotions "positively" impart their influence to make us more in-touch human beings. It is not *what* we feel that declares our character but rather our conduct in the midst of *whatever* we feel (Morita, 1928/1998, p. 7). You happen upon a stranger prostrate in the blistering heat. Do you give water or not? Whatever you feel at that moment is less critical than the act itself. Acting generously, in fact, helps to stir feelings of compassion. But giving water that is desperately needed does not have to wait for compassion to be felt. *There are no positive or negative emotions, only positive or negative behavior.*

Aristotle

Just as we do not dictate emotions, they also do not have power over us. Aristotle, in *Nicomachean Ethics*, writes that anyone can become angry — that's easy. But to be angry with the right person, to the right degree, at the right time, for the right purpose, in the right way – this is not easy (Goleman, 1997, p. ix). There are two conspicuous references here: one to the *feeling* of anger (anyone can become angry) and the other to the *outpouring* of anger (angry with the right person, etc.). All of us can and have experienced the emotion of anger. As Morita (1928/1998) counsels, a person cannot avoid feeling anger (e.g., when someone speaks ill of her/him) yet can refrain from *quarreling* over the matter (p. 72). For the Japanese, showing anger and irritability are anathema because they disrupt the social order. Japanese hence define virtue by (1) the ability to control impulsive behavior; (2) motivation to do what is right; and (3) adroitness in interpersonal relationships.

The Japanese adhere to *enryo*: outward reserve in certain social interactions to forego upsetting displays of emotions. This self-discipline is a response to the endless needs to reconcile the different spheres of mutual obligations, respect, and nurturance (Kirmayer, 2002, p. 308). According to Doi (1977), there are three concentric circles of *enryo*: the inner circle of relatives and the outer circle of strangers where no *enryo* is necessary, and the middle circle of acquaintances at work or in the community where circumspect behavior is mandatory. This "(over)sensitive forethought," because of elevated concern for the evaluation of others in this middle circle, makes possible the public spirit of diffidence. It also in part explains why so many Japanese are plagued by stifling self-consciousness.

Assay this rationalization: "I am too shy to ask for a date." The risk of rejection or embarrassment can be intimidating and set off bouts of shyness. Shyness can result in a variety of problems, including low self-esteem, loneliness, depression, and isolation (Ishiyama, 1987). Always having to assume a secure self-image in front of others may interfere with being socially engaging even if a person possesses sufficient interpersonal skills (Nakamura, Kitanishi, & Ushijima, 1994, p. 149). *Asking* for a date, notwithstanding, is behavior. Shyness does *not* preclude taking initiative. Feeling shy or not, we ask for the date if it is "the right person," "the right time," "for the right purpose," and "in the right way." We do not wait for shyness to melt away. If we pay attention to when and how we ask rather than our emotions before and during asking, our chances of succeeding are far greater.

Although types of social interactions differ culturally, and deviations from the norm cannot be defined universally (Tarumi, Ichimiya, Yamada, Umesue, & Kuroki, 2004), everyone feels inadequate in some social situations. In certain individuals, however, strong social anxiety and self-focus produce unrelieved *taijin-kyofu-sho*: literally, the disorder (*sho*) of fear (*kyofu*) of interpersonal relationships (*taijin*). Ashamed about awkward demeanor and obsessed with their "repulsive" physical characteristics, these persons feel unacceptable, despised, and avoided by others (Maeda & Nathan, 1999, p. 525; Nakamura, Kitanishi, Miyake, Hashimoto, & Kubota, 2002, p. 595).

Morita therapy addresses social phobia by helping clients immerse in behaviors that transcend their symptoms in order to have them experience their behavioral potentials (Ishiyama, 1987, p. 547). The Morita premise is that social anxiety has a self-actualizing value, and thus can be used as a motivator-facilitator rather than an inhibitor of meaningful action. The desire for social success is expressed in the fear of social ineptitude. Public self-consciousness and fear of negative evaluation are not the problems. It is the negative processing of this experience resulting in behavioral passivity. There is, in fact, a useful quality to the social sensitivity underneath the social anxiety. Ishiyama (1987, p. 549) writes that shyness and nervousness in social situations make us careful not to say hurtful or disconcerting things to others or to make social blunders.

Hairy caterpillar

Morita (1928/1998) notes the revulsion a person might feel upon seeing a hairy caterpillar on the kitchen table. The revulsion is an *emotional fact*. To remove the caterpillar is a *reasonable response*. The attempt to eliminate the uncomfortable feeling *before* acting creates fertile conditions for the formation of obsessive disorders (p. 6). Ishiyama (1990) explains that while cognitive behaviorists tend to engage clients in altering cognitions (e.g., rational self-talk about the caterpillar's harmlessness) to legislate affective responses, such attempts are considered by Moritists to be "self-focusing and self-defeating" (p. 566). Behavioral therapists also often use systematic desensitization and dosed exposure, combining relaxation/relief and gradual/interval introduction to fears (Spates, 2004). Morita therapists instead help clients to focus on their self-actualizing desires (a caterpillar-free table) and ability to choose actions (removal of the caterpillar). The escalated emotional symptoms (revulsion at the caterpillar being on the table) are left to a natural healing process.

Another example would be quavering about traveling on an airplane. We do not rehearse the middling steps — buying a ticket, sitting at the airport, and boarding a flight — in order to overcome this fear. Oblique experimentation is only slightly helpful. We fly, tremulous or not, in order to forthrightly meet our professional or personal obligations. Feelings are *not* directly under our control; we therefore are *not* responsible for what we feel. The actions we take, however, are controllable with very few exceptions. Emotions do not cause, enable, or prevent us from doing what is proper. Welding our emotional state to behavior to justify our action or inaction is unproductive. We do not have to be stymied by having to like what we do or doing only what we like. We either act or not act. There are some plainspoken Moritists who insist that there is no obscuring of responsibility such as "I *try* to be honest." We are honest or we are not honest. In the words of Hasegawa (1993):

> *Kanjo ni sekinin ha naiga.*
> *Kodo niha sekinin ga aru.*
>
> Feeling does not have responsibility.
> Behavior has responsibility.

(p. 4)

The disentanglement of emotion and behavior helps sort out what we are experiencing. Bereavement, for example, over a valid loss is healthy. Feeling sad and reacting sensitively to the death of loved ones are unavoidable. They are as natural as water flowing to lower latitude (Morita, 1928/1998, p. 19). In Japanese culture, sadness and grief are positively valued: the Japanese draw strength from these experiences, tighten their bond with those among the living, and reaffirm group solidarity (Kirmayer, 2002, p. 305). Lock (1993, pp. 222-223), moreover, characterizes the Japanese as on occasion *welcoming* sadness and melancholy for their symbolic value: a reminder of the ephemeral nature of human life.

Experiencing grief in all its powerful aspects, regardless, is different from *dwelling* in grief. We can unreservedly mourn because any emotion's natural course is "parabolic": it flares up, reaches a climax, then lessens and disappears (Morita, 1928/1998, p. 31). Consequently, we are unburdened from dragging around hefty and ever-piling emotional baggage throughout our lives. If a particular disturbing emotion does reappear again and again, this could be a "signpost" of an ineffective lifeway and the need to modify what we are doing. As Morita (Matesz, 1990) noted, emotions may be valuable indicators of the extent to which we are living "creatively and benevolently" (p. 20). If we are regularly disgruntled, for example, in our job or marriage, it may signal the time to seek career or marital counseling. Habitual complaining, however, can also indicate that we have built a "castle of egocentric emotions" (Morita, 1928/1998, p. 16). Fault-finding has become dominant in our lives, and our judgment of facts is distorted.

Two wings of desire

A Chinese proverb goes: "We do not live for a hundred years but worry enough for a thousand" (Char, 1970, p. 15). Worrying, according to Morita (Osumi & Miyasato, 2004; Nakamura, 1989), is profuse with no qualitative differences between a neurotic and healthy person. Kora (1989) adds that not only is generalized anxiety common to all people, it originates secondarily to the more fundamental "desire for life" (*sei no yokubo*) that any person has without exception.

> *Fuan to kibou ha yokubou no ryoyoku.*
>
> Our desire has two wings.
> One is anxiety.
> The other is hope.
>
> (Hasegawa, 1993, p. 9)

The originality of Morita theory is that it attributes the cause of neurosis to the *secondary* meanings which are attached to emotional reactions and not to the onset of the emotions themselves. When a person becomes perturbed about the original disturbance, a "double suffering" develops (LeVine, 1993, p. 84). This happens, for example, when we engulf ourselves with anxiety about everything, worry about the fact we are worrying (*tokeware*), or attempt to become worry-free. Worry becomes problematic when it smothers the focus to adapt or improvise to the instant situation (Frager, u.d., p. 52). It is what we *do* with our anxiety that affects our creativity and productiveness and *not* the anxiety itself.

Individuals, for example, enter into relationships for a variety of purposes, and when those purposes are fulfilled or gone, the relationships end (Millman, 1992, p. 31). Nonetheless, separation or divorce can be a harrowing experience. Despite compelling reasons for the dissolution of the marriage, there may be innumerable uncertainties about financial, family, and legal matters. This natural anxiety does not have to imperil decision-making. Anxiety can help spell out the foremost things in our lives that merit planning and follow-through. As Morita (1928/1998) stated, worries are prerequisites for the realization of human desire (p. 87). The stronger is our desire for a successful life, the stronger our anxiety. The more we judge the consequences to be costly and permanent, the more we invest greater anxiety in the unknown: "Will my decisions be sensible and astute or ill-advised and petulant?"

Tuyoi fuan ha tuyoi yokubo.

Strong anxiety is strong desire.
(Hasegawa, 1993, p. 13)

As Kora (1989) states, anxiety is wholesome as a "motivational force toward self-actualization" (p. 79). It goads us to stay on task and be more scrupulous decision-makers. One Morita client shared that his anxieties make him more thoroughly prepare for his daily work. By also leaving the symptoms of his anxiety as they are, he is less careless while working. The client was not cured by overcoming anxiety but by recognizing its true meaning and usefulness (Kora, 1967, pp. 92). Anxiety proves that we have valued interests and expectations. Like a sopping and cumbersome waterbag, we lug around anxiety in the "thirst to live." We do not shield ourselves from disappointment by averting risk-taking and diminishing our ambition. We are not impervious because there are things worth fretting over!

Fumon

Panic attacks are the crescendo from being swept up in self-defeating, despotic beliefs about how "I should feel" or "I must be." This overperfectionism, self or coercively imposed, tightens the grip of anxiety until it snaps in acute cognitive desperation and/or somatic upheaval (e.g., the "hysterical ball" in the throat, chest pain, or gastric spasms). In subsequent similar contexts, focusing on the fearsomeness of a previous panic attack, a person cannot make calm observations and reenacts the past experience of pain in the present reality (Morita, 1928/1998, pp. 113-114). These persons, Morita argued, live entirely in a subjective-centered world and have no room for anything else. They may feel pain when pricked with a pin but feel nothing when witnessing another person being pierced by a spear. Just as a starving person rarely feeds others, persons with anxiety-based disorders have no room to care for others, because they feel overwhelmed by their own suffering and fear (p. 116).

The way to free oneself from a panic attack is mindful engagement in practical thinking and action (Azuma, 2001). Nakamura (u.d.) writes that anxiety will soon peak and ease if one holds the anxiety without trying to manage the way out of it. By leaving anxiety as it is, one is liberated to exert the desire for life behind the anxiety through constructive behaviors (p. 2). Morita therapists, accordingly, adopt *fumon* ('disregarding method" or "strategic inattention"). The causes and symptoms of anxiety are not directly addressed (Nakamura, 2004). The goal is to improve functioning in real life, a holistic or context-based approach, rather than self-centered mental health per se (Matsuda, 2004). Emphasis is placed upon what can be realistically accomplished in any given situation. As Kitanishi and Mori (1995) explain, the goal of an anxiety-free existence is equivalent to being "irresponse-able" to the meaningful aspects of our lives. It is not how well we "manage" anxiety and worry but how well we manage life.

As a university professor, the week before I administer a major examination, many students implore me to divulge a few of the test questions to help ease their intensifying anxiety. I tell the students to appreciate anxiety because it is an ally of their goal to learn. They should *exploit* the anxiety to reinforce their focus on study. As Jinsheng (2004) argues, there is "an intelligence derived from anxiety." The indifferent students, on the other hand, are stress-free because they are not particularly invested in their performance on the exam. These students do not have the advantage of anxiety. As Pinker (2004) states, "Anxiety is an impetus to avoid invisible threats, and most of us would never meet a deadline without it" (p. 78).

Merging Currents: As we become more accepting of all our emotions, we must strengthen our sense of responsibility for what we do or do not do.

Chapter 9

Morita Life Principle Nine
Success

"Life flows from being response-able"

As an old saying goes, "Even steel
gathers rust, if it is not used."
Shoma Morita
(1928/1998, p. 115)

Bursting out

In traditional residential Morita therapy, an initial period of individual bedrest for 7-10 days is prescribed for those found suitable after strict screening for psychosis, suicidal ideology, and antisocial behavior (Morita, 1928/1998, pp. 36-52). In compact, private rooms with only *tatami* and *futon* for furnishings, patients are instructed to quietly and conscientiously reflect upon their distress. Reading, smoking, listening to the radio, writing, engaging in hobbies, or any other pastime is not permitted. Leaving the room is allowed only for brief visits to nearby washrooms. The time is to be spent lying in bed thinking whatever thoughts come to mind and feeling whatever feelings occur. Staff members deliver nourishing meals on trays without fanfare or discourse. Patients are informed that they might feel bored during the course of bedrest, because doing nothing may seem unbearable or even ridiculous. How can cure come from lying in bed? Patients may even have the urge to leave the hospital, but are told to accept bedrest "as a duty" whatever mood grips them (Kora, 1968, p. 625).

At first, many patients are relieved to enter into an extended period of respite, recuperation (*yojo*), and rumination. Although a mental matrix of potential solutions may take form, within a few days most patients catch that no amount of painstaking thinking resolves their life problems. They become mentally and emotionally depleted as alternating periods of drowsiness and restlessness set in. As one patient, in retrospect, described his sixth day of bedrest, "I had nothing more to think about . . . I had no way of passing the long day doing nothing . . . I was now at wit's end" (Kora, 1965, p. 625).

Patients eventually begin to covet placing their ideas into practice to verify prospective remedies in everyday living. Confinement, however, postpones any real action so that patients search for ways to help break the tedium of waiting. As Morita (1928/1998) noted, "Healthy minds do not tolerate boredom; thinking and acting simply occur" (p. 40). Activity, however, does not exist for the purpose of escaping boredom. Boredom exists, as Frankl (1955) argued, so that "we will escape inactivity and do justice to the meaning of our life" (p. 87).

When we are unusually sedentary within a narcissistic "exaggerated self," our overall wellbeing suffers (LeVine, 2004). The fewer our activities, the less responsibilities we hold. The fewer our responsibilities, the less commitments we make. The fewer our commitments, the less we participate in life. The human body, psyche, and soul crave *prompting*. Patients in absolute bedrest, consequently, after having saturated themselves with self-focus, begin to observe facets of their living quarters they have previously overlooked. Details of the walls and ceiling become conspicuous: shades of color, design irregularities, assorted shapes, and unusual angles. The yearning to engage something, anything, tilts toward an appreciation of the once ignored or taken-for-granted. Patients take crisp note of the chirping birds in the outside garden; newly relish the taste, texture, and display of the meals brought to them; indulge in the heretofore nuisance of washroom visits; and boost their physical movement. The body, having been restricted, aches to "burst out." As one patient announced:

> I feel like a child now . . . I feel an irresistible urge to do something . . . I can see Mt. Fuji, I can see the bus, the clear sky. Never did the world look so pretty to me in my life."
> (Kora, 1968, p. 626).

Falling chrysanthemum

LeVine (2004) states that the period of absolute bedrest serves to center the patient on her/his own experience: "Silence is the stepping stone that prepares one to return to all of one's senses . . . (and) set the stage for desire to emerge in exaggerated forms." Periods of light and heavy work and re-socialization into the community then logically follow bedrest. Patients are guided to do routine chores around the residence, including cooking, cleaning, and gardening. They are not to do this just to be active but to appreciate not dirtying things, preparing good food, and being unself-consciously helpful to one another.

Patients are not made to do work by the therapist but do so voluntarily and spontaneously (C. Fujita, personal communication, October 20, 2004): "Listen to the need and act!" "Please act to find your own work!" If a stalk of chrysanthemum, for example, is falling, then the opportunity is born to give it support (Reynolds, 1976, p. 31). As the saying goes, "Before enlightenment: chop wood, carry water. After enlightenment: chop wood, carry water" (Morita, 1928/1998, p. 96). Work is done, in other words, when it hooks our attention and needs to be done, whether or not we (pre)judge it to be "interesting" or "enjoyable." Work is good in and of itself, benefits the individual and society, and liberates the self-centered person (Reynolds, 1976, p. 32). Morita therapy, in this manner, provides a disciplined training period of parting from a self-involved life to "matter-centered" living (Kitanishi & Mori, 1995).

As we exert this *rhythm in daily living* without partiality to emotional payback or stoppage by neurotic symptoms, we become more prolific and aware of our desire to live fully. This is similar to the artist who is blending colors with a brush. Deeply focusing on the shades of colors, the artist becomes unhindered by the shades of her or his emotions. The artist's full creativity depends upon transcending ego and defocusing on emotion-prompted actions (LeVine, 1993, p. 84).

Kodo ga mugen no kanosei o hiraku.

Behavior makes possibility endless.
(Hasegawa, 1993, p. 10)

We of course need periodic reevaluation of what we are doing *in*, *for*, and *to* our lives. If we never pause, we will not recognize what we need to put a stop to in our lives. Self-reflection reins us in from being too frivolous and jumbled. Ellis (1996), for example, conjectures that we can control an emotional reaction to an activating event by how we think about that event through "cognitive restructuring." Disputation of old beliefs about ourselves and acquisition of new ones may be a palliative, but a scrutinized life itself is impotent. When we are compelled by the whole of our being — not just by our rationality — we undividedly experience the desire for life and are able to intuitively follow its natural course (Nakamura, et al., 1994, p. 151).

Everyday enlightenment

Gustave Flauber, in his 19th Century masterpiece *Madame Bovary*, wrote cynically about the "insufficiency of life" when even happiness is more tinsel than gold and a cheap and ugly lie: "Nothing was worth the trouble of seeking it . . . Every smile hid a yawn of boredom, every joy a curse, all pleasure satiety, and the sweetest kisses left upon your lips only the unattainable desire for a greater delight." Notwithstanding Flauber's diatribe, optimists probably do fare better than pessimists. Western cognitive therapy, for that reason, teaches reframing of thoughts in order to disintegrate destructive patterns of behavior. Byrne (2006), a popular writer on the metaphysical, moreover, believes that a secret, cosmic "law of attraction" is tapped when we exude positive images of the health, wealth, and relationships that we desire. We become irresistible magnets that pull what we want in life towards us. Starting on something small like finding a parking space, we move on to bigger things like winning the lottery!

Morita (1928/1998), while he did instruct his clients to have a "proper mental attitude," emphasized that sometimes we are positive about life and sometimes we are not. The mind is always changing as circumstances change. It is like a mirror: things are reflected when they come in front of it and disappear when they pass by it. Our thoughts therefore usually occur randomly and cannot be managed at will. They come and go, but we don't always have to let them take us with them (cf. Needleman in Hammond & Ferguson, 1998, p. 76). We can only find "true peace of mind" by accepting that life is alternately bitter and sweet (Morita, 1928/1998, p. 87). We will then be guided between fatalistic pessimism ("there is no good") and unremitting optimism ("there is no bad").

Mental activity, Morita (1928/1998) argued, is only controlled by volition when our minds are working toward a purposeful goal (p. 13). He thus guided his clients to practice correct habits and healthy activities. What counts is what we do regardless of the transitory state of our thinking. As Millman (1992) states, "Just as our life is starting to get better, we may feel like things are getting worse — because for the first time we see clearly what needs to be done" (p. 15). Despite what Byrne (2006) preaches, it is thus more likely that we gain what we desire because we approach our "happiness quotients" and life's possibilities with more consciousness and receptivity. Those matters and things that have meaning for us are themselves the magnetic force that snags our attention and energy. It is working through the medium of action rather than positive thinking itself that overcomes undesirable, impoverished, or harsh realities.

Andrew Vachss (2002), for example, a New York lawyer whose only clients are children, is outspoken against those who viciously prey on them. The fundamental question, according to Vachss, is whether or not these child predators are ailing *or* evil. Merely identifying the rape, torture, and murder of children as sickening and malevolent, however, makes little difference. Until we act, Vachss pleads, nothing will change! Paul Loeb (1999), furthermore, an authority on the psychology of human involvement, often writes about benevolence in a time of pandemic cynicism. The times may be spinning toward catastrophe — instability wrought by international conflicts and environmental non-sustainability — but it is unambiguous service that evinces our humanity in spite of the prospects. The difference between "activism" and "quietism," in fact, may not be opposing philosophy as much as personal temperament. Social activists may just be more inclined to interfere than quietists who seek cooperation, evolvement, and deliberation (Smullyan, 1977, pp. 148-149). Humanitarianism, aside from its mode, is measured by effect more than affect.

Everything matters

Japanese samurai personified that the self-discipline required of mastery inseminates every action (Hyams, 1979, p. 15). As Bruce Lee (1975) explained, the development of our "natural weapons" is not to hurt someone but to overcome our own greed, anger, and folly to become fully aware and calm (p. 13). This is the transcendence of a particular art or pursuit to mastery of oneself (Frager, u.d., p. 68). According to the classic Zen saying, "Do everything as you do anything." Just as we can ascertain the growth of trees by studying acorns and shrubs, the proficiency to meet epic life tasks is predicated in the performance of modest ones.

This is the gist of the dictum: "Never trust a simple meal to a simple cook." The more simple is the dish, the less the margin for error in execution. Food critic Mimi Sheraton (2002) asserts that nowhere is this more apparent than in microcosmical Japanese sushi. What could be more innocent than pressing a slice of raw fish onto a morsel of rice, then dabbing on a bit of *wasabi* ("Japanese horseradish") and a drop of *murasaki* ("soy sauce for sushi")? This elemental combination, however, fits the Japanese genius for making much out of little through aesthetic enhancement. Everything matters with sushi: the fish and its slicing and handling; the rice and its preparation and seasoning; the quality of the *nori* ("seaweed"); the harmony between the food and the dishes it's served on; the décor and ambiance of the dining room; and, most critically, the skill and demeanor of the *itamae* ("sushi chef") (p. 90).

Japanese food generally lacks the intensity of flavor of other Asian cuisines. Spices and garlic are hardly ever used. The barely perceptible differences in flavor between varieties of raw fish (sashimi) are prized by the Japanese. Subtleties between virtually "tasteless" dishes, not tampered with by lavish sauces, test the fineness of a person's palate (Keene, 1989, p. 133). Perfection in sushi and life, in other words, derives from attention to the fine points. The capacity to respond appropriately to *anything* we face in life is advanced in *everything* we responsibly do.

Traditional motor learning theory emphasized that skill learning is specific to the context and task performed. Deftly hammering a nail had little to do with squarely driving home an argument. Recent data, however, show that acquired expertise is much more transferable (Seidler, 2004). Practicing one kind of skill helps to develop other skills. Skill-building fundamentals — concentration, form, timing, and force — are *identical* in kind and cumulative for broadening capabilities. The human brain is not a fixed mass that shapes behavior but a net of neuropathways spawned by multiple behaviors. We can "cross-train the brain" to become more productive (Yang & Useem, 2006).

Multitasking

The air-traffic controllers at our nation's busiest airports undertake awesome responsibility for the safety of millions of travelers. They are consummate multitaskers. Ceaselessly scanning blinking radar screens, controllers must correctly guide a menagerie of aircraft at terminal gates or on crisscross runways, authorizing a flurry of arrivals and departures. They must listen and reply to dissonant radio transmissions; monitor weather patterns and ground conditions; and make split-second decisions in emergencies. Their work is uncommonly stressful.

Multitasking, nevertheless, is *not* managing many competing demands *at once*. From ancient times we have known this to be unfeasible: "To do two things at once is to do neither" (Publius, circa 42 BC). Multitasking is the ability to concentrate on a *single task* (among many) at the *precise moment* it is the most "urgent." This is *timing*, the capacity to choose for principal effect the salient moment for taking specific action so as to smoothly integrate the task and the next, and so forth. Our awareness is set for other pending tasks, but each of these does not fully occupy our attention and response until instantly necessary. Otherwise, we would end up with a collection of haphazard actions, most of which would be insufficiently completed.

Ima dekirukotoha hitotu shikanai.

The thing we can do now is only one thing.
(Hasegawa, 1993, p. 11)

Multitasking is hence the judicious shifting of attention in a seamless "taskstream" that meets the need to do this one thing at this moment and do it well without complication or redundancy. This temporal processing depends upon the auditory, visual, and tactile neural framework that has been encoded by focused action (Karmarkar & Buonomano, 2007). As we are paying attention, in other words, each moment bids us to act. To break the sense of being overwhelmed with too many things pulling from too many directions, we need only to trust the most apparent.

Multitasking is therefore the offspring of *fluency*, *forthrightness*, and *flexibility*. The poet Su Tung-po (Smullyan, 1997), for example, represents the arduous and multifaceted task of writing as the "inexhaustible spring" that spreads out everywhere over the countryside. The words surge along the level ground, "flowing with ease a thousand *li* in a single day." When they encounter hills and boulders, bends and turns, they take form according to the things about them. The words are not logorrheic, but "always go and stop where they should" (pp. 158-159).

Carried by a current

Mihaly Csikszentmihalyi of the University of Chicago asked 100,000 individuals around the country to wear pocket pagers. They were assigned to write down what they were feeling whenever the pager randomly signaled. When what the subjects were doing was going exceedingly well, they reported a state like "being carried by a current." They had a clear sense of what they had to do moment by moment, regardless of the type of activity. Csikszentmihalyi (1990) refers to this as "optimal experience." It is not a passive state ("going with the flow") but an active building of a fulfilling life ("creative flow"). This "thin moment" is the heightened performance zone to which superb athletes refer. It is the flow where doing is not encumbered with overanalysis.

From a Moritist perspective, weak vitality coupled with low concentration inhibits living. Such an individual would be sallow and lackluster. High energy, however, welded to inattentiveness produces a chaotic life. Absence of vigor paired with stanch attention results in a narrow-focused personality. The most powerful life flow occurs when infinite drive and purposeful attention intersect.

* * * * * * * * * * * * * * * *

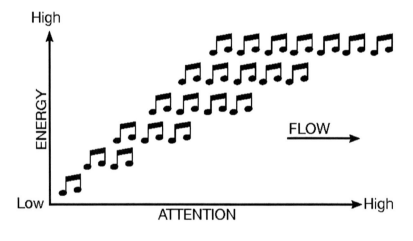

Living in flow is like beautiful singing: the intuitive, pitch-perfect vocalizing of successive notes. The next step or decision in our lives naturally proceeds as we are "in tune" with our innate energy and life purposes. This echoes the Chinese Taoist concept of *wei-wu-wei* ("effortless action" or "not forcing"). We only do what is necessary and natural: allowing ourselves to be guided by life's unfolding, and refining our objectives and applying our determination accordingly. It is the "labor of love" that never seems like effort at all (cf. Smullyan, 1977, p, 161). As Dillard (quoted by Heat-Moon, 2001) writes, the secret is "to sail on a solar wind." We hone and spread our spirit until we ourselves are a sail, "whetted, translucent, broadside to the merest puff." Self-consciousness recedes ("we ourselves are a sail") as we become one with what we are doing ("broadside to the merest puff") (p. 70). We are free from the dualism of an actor and the action. There is *only* the act.

While in this flow we may be tremendously stretching and wholly exerting ourselves. The *kiai* during *kumite* ("sparring") or *kata* ("form") in martial arts is the "cry which gives life." It is the art of perfectly concentrating all of our energy upon a given object to achieve our goal. Upon completion of the *kumite* or *kata* (or any activity), we feel relaxed and fulfilled. As Csikszentmihalyi (1990) discovered in his research, a great concentration occurs when we feel that what we can do and what has to be done are more or less in balance. Having too many challenges does not overwhelm us, nor are we bored by having too few things to do.

Monkey bars

In the 1980s, building self-esteem in students took precedence in the American educational system. Educators surmised that if students felt good about themselves, they would improve at spelling and arithmetic as well as become more productive in general. To the contrary, "feeling better" did not automatically bring about higher school achievement or first-class citizenry. The emphasis on self-worth, in fact, seemed to jeopardize success in academic and social areas. As a result, there was a reemphasis on the rudiments of education and skills building. As Stevens (1998) contends, there is nothing that boosts self-concept more than being able to do something—it doesn't matter if it's reading or something on the monkey bars your brother can't do. Morita (1928/1998) alike remarked that we can cultivate courage and self-confidence only through repeated experiences and successes. We then become accustomed to the pain that accompanies diligence and learn the pleasure of success (p. 33).

Educators by the same token must cast their teaching in *behavior* rather than feelings toward their students. Kora (1990) describes how a Morita therapist counseled a schoolteacher who believed that he had to impartially love all of his students. Because some of the students were repugnant to him, the teacher began to deride himself and hate his profession. The therapist's counsel to the teacher was that it is only human nature to have different feelings about his students. The repulsive children also must be taught well, even if he did not like to do so, because he was entrusted with their education, too. If he maintained this approach, he "may come to love those children for whom he felt only aversion in the beginning" (pp. 12-13).

Mind of a sage

There is a saying that a servant maddening dashes to and fro but a king serenely reposes in his palace. For many, the pace of society is both quickening and enslaving. Craving membership in the monoculture of prosperity, we speed race to succeed (cf. Kirmayer, 2002, p. 316). We are enamored by the clout, prestige, and competitiveness of those who have accumulated more than they can ever spend or need. As "voyeurs of billionaires" (Goolsbee, 2007) material excess has become our metronome of modern living. Seductive commercialism sustained by calculated obsolescence entice us to purchase the in vogue and chic without charity to those who lack even the bygone and outworn.

As Ernest Callenbach (2000), author of *Living Cheaply in Style*, contends, we live in "trance of consumerism." We forthwith need to decelerate, buy less, save more, and recycle! This voluntary simplicity includes avoidance of many possessions irrelevant to the chief purpose of life—allowing restraint in some directions in order to secure abundance in other directions. Kenkō (1283-1350) thus wrote that it is excellent for one to be simple in tastes and to avoid extravagance, for "the wise are rarely rich" (Keene, 1989, p. 133). Morita (1928/1998) as well pointed out that the mind of the common person is aroused by gain, while that of a sage awakens to justice (p. 119).

The practice of simplicity is reified in traditional Zen monasteries where monks vow to remain "uncarved blocks" (Ives, 1992). The personal possessions of monks are austere: a cushion, bedroll, robes, sandals, bowls, chopsticks, and toilet articles. Unadorned robes are sewn from rags scavenged and dyed by neophytes before their ordination. Nothing is wasted: all food is eaten, the little garbage goes to the compost pile, and human excrement is used for fertilizer. Spoken words are sparing and chatter is nonexistent.

Inversely, when we enjoy more than we actually need, our notion of what constitutes living well bumps up. We then suffer "collapse anxiety," the fear that we will somehow lose what we have gained (Easterbrook, 2004). Life, by most socio-economic measures, is better for most Americans but many feel worse! Permeating materialism appears not to slake our truest needs and brings its own misery and pathologies. As Kirmayer (2002, p. 317) posits, dysphoria and depression may point to problems not in brain chemistry but *in the way we live*.

Falling ahead

Many of us are not calcified by the dearth of choices in life but an oversupply. We invest too much time trying to make the right choice and later too much time regretting having made the wrong choice. Blunders in career, family, and work can be ruefully unnerving, compounding into petrifying self-doubt (cf. Schwartz, 2004). If we are standing at a personal crossroad, however, dismayed as to the direction to take, we need to move down the path judged to be the best *at the time*. If we are observant, we will soon know whether or not we chose wisely. If so, we can continue. If not, we can set out on an alternate path, *adjusting as we proceed*. What lies ahead can only become less ambiguous by not deferring action. There is the adage: "If you don't know where you are going, any road will take you there." Moritists would more readily counsel: "Walk well the road you are on and you will find where you are going."

There is really no falling behind if we trust "falling ahead" (cf. Levine, 2004). The pouring of ourselves into an activity at hand with full attention has at minimum trickle-down benefits: the quality of our actions increases. Even if we start something that we have never done before, no matter how poorly it turns out, we are on our way to doing it better the next time. Ives (1992, p. 35) suggests, therefore, that we avoid the awful confusion that occurs with swirling thoughts: we fail to concentrate and scramble to do several things at once. As Zenists admonish, "If you walk, just walk. If you sit, just sit. Don't wobble!"

Nevertheless, many of us — even with incumbent motivation and behavioral range to do what needs to be done — do not take action. Anxious perfectionists are convinced that they must wait for the right mood, mental confidence, and conducive environment to act. Ishiyama (1990), for example, writes of a college student who tried to make herself feel inspired to write two overdue papers. She tried to meditate to calm herself and not be distracted. She rearranged her study room to feel prepared to work, did extra reading to feel self-confident, and snacked frequently when feeling restless. All had failed.

Ishiyama asked the student to accept that inconvenient feelings are an inevitable part of the process of facing demanding tasks and stressful situations. Trying to fight or manipulate these emotions and imperfect subjective states are like the donkey in the Zen story of *keroketsu* referenced by Morita. Tied to a post the donkey tries to free itself by moving around the post until it ends up being immobilized by its own actions (Ishiyama, 1990, p. 567). The student, by attempting to escape fears and discomfort through self-defeating means, only became more ensnared in her suffering. She had, in fact, scapegoated her inner conflicts as the reason for not completing her assignments. Kora (Ishiyama, 1990) referred to this as "defensive oversimplification" (p. 568).

The student was instructed to generate short draft-quality papers and then convert them into final products over several days, leaving behind the ineffective strategy of inducing ideal mental and emotional conditions. As she tackled her priorities, they no longer haunted her. She could, in Morita's words, "succeed while failing" (Reynolds, 1984, p. 97), because her *behavioral momentum* — from brief drafts to full essays — stripped away resistance to move ahead (cf. Nevin, Mandell, & Atak, 1983). In classical physics, momentum is velocity multiplied by mass. In life, momentum is achieved through well-timed actions reinforced by discipline. Adding sides to a polygon may never produce a full circle, but it more and more becomes like one (cf. Ives, 1992, p. 70).

Ikigai Ryoho

The human condition is inevitably marked by illness, aging, and death. As Buddhism teaches, suffering does not come directly from these realities but from our natural fears about them (Kirmayer, 2002, p. 309; Morita, 1928/1998, p. 95). This dread is the companion to passion for life. What we fear to lose, therefore, must not be sacrificed to that fear. The prevailing notion that when something becomes broken or old, it becomes obsolete and disposable only worsens our misgivings. Ram Dass (A. Gross, 2000), alternatively, has said that infirmities offer the chance to let go of the compulsion to "keep busy" and instead "tune in to the richness of the moment." Our culture sees life as collecting experiences, but aging is an emptying out and experiencing what's happening right now. Ram Dass submits that our culture mistakenly values old people who act young rather than old people for acting old, for their wisdom (A. Gross, 2000, pp. 12, 14, 16; Ram Dass, 2001, p. 18).

Growing old can be *growing* old. We can still generate personal growth by disencumbering from certain activities in favor of others (cf. Albom, 1997, p. 118). Jinro Itami, a Moritist physician and founder of *Ikigai Ryoho* (Meaningful Life Therapy) counsels his terminal cancer patients to leave something useful for society rather than merely seek to set their minds at rest (Ishiyama, 1990, p. 83). Buford (2004) hails this as "socially productive aging." In aging and dying we must continue to value life and do our utmost. As Ishiyama (1990, p. 78) writes, those with intractable diseases can be helped not by religious conversion, a stoic philosophy, optimism through positive thinking, or death education. Instead, patients need to acquire practical tools which they can use to stay alive mentally and physically and to carve out meaning from their present life.

Itami's challenge is succinct: "You may be physically sick, but do not become a sick person" (Ishiyama, 1990, p. 79). The end of our lives is not like water feebly draining into a standpipe. We can be a co-catalyst of disease management rather than a phlegmatic depot of medical care. We can prepare for death by writing a will and handling unfinished business (Ishiyama, 1990, pp. 79-80). We can set immediate goals and do something each day for the benefit of others and contribute to our own wellbeing (Itami, 2004). Liebenberg (Nakamura, u.d.), a Moritist social worker at Memorial Sloan-Kettering Cancer Center in New York, refers to this as the balancing of "self-preservation" (fighting against disease) and "self-development" (striving for enrichment) (p. 4).

Itami (1990) teaches us to be pupils of those terminally ill virtuosos who live their lives to their fullest potentials, welcoming ever-greater meaning in life until their last living moment. There is acting response-able and irresponse-able in *every* stage and condition of life. Harayda (2004), for example, writes that she tries not to dwell on the "imponderable question" as to why her brother died soon after surviving the attacks on the World Trade Center. Instead, she focuses on what he did in the time he had. Some have expressed to Harayda how much more good her brother could have done if he had lived longer, but Harayda replies that she thinks of "how much *less* good he could have done if he had died sooner" (p. 14).

Merging Currents: We must seek balance in how much and in what areas we expend ourselves.

Chapter 10

Morita Life Principle Ten Balance

"Life flows from being centered"

Healthy individuals have a wide range of abilities for meeting the demands of daily living; they adapt themselves readily to change, develop themselves, and respond to other people. Health is not based on a single characteristic, such as having a sound body, good memory, or vivid imagination.

Shoma Morita
(1928/1998, p. 132)

Moderation

Morita Therapy was formally introduced into China in 1980 and has gained wide acceptance there (Cui, 2004). Chinese Moritists especially note the native ties of Morita principles to Chinese Taoism (Wang, 2004). One of the basic tenets of Taoism is the comparison of nature's course to a bow: that which is at the top is pulled down, and that which is at the bottom is brought up; that which is overfull is reduced, and that which is deficient is supplemented (Loy, 1985). Nature is a succession of alternations: when an extreme is approached, a reversal occurs. Those who abide in the Tao therefore know when to stop, and are free from the dangers of extremes. *Over*doing or *under*doing instills harm, but moderation in all aspects of life secures maximum health and wellness. Our *chi* ("vital energy") is then unconstrained in its flow.

Morita (1928/1998, p. 20) equally wrote that "self-inhibitory" or "self-harmonizing" processes are inherent to how we ideally function as humans. Having self-esteem is natural but not self-scorn *or* self-aggrandizement. Labor validates but not laziness *or* overwork. Humor uplifts but not morbidity *or* mischief. That is, a confident, active, and amusing person is considerably more alive (and more likeable!) than the person who limps in self-hatred, sloth, and foreboding *or* who exudes arrogance, greediness, and malice.

This natural "opposing function" makes possible movement toward a healthy life. When this counterbalancing process, however, is *deficient*, impulsive and imprudent behaviors are exhibited (such as alcohol abuse or drug addiction). When the self-inhibitory function is *overpowering*, spontaneity is lost (such as in chronic depression or catatonic schizophrenia). As Xinli (2004) states, this is like a person trying to walk on one leg: unsteadiness and awkwardness abound. Menter (2003), for example, writes about a friend who was stressed-out over a particularly trying situation at her job. This friend had examined the problem from every possible angle, but couldn't stop feeling furious. She painfully asked Menter, "What am I to do about a situation like this?" Menter responded, "Why not think about what you want to have for lunch?" The friend was at first taken aback and then grew silent. "You know," she said after a moment, "I think that's the single best piece of advice anyone's ever given me." At any given moment, she could disconnect from her tangled feelings and focus on something more benign. She did not have to keep stampeding her problem in the same "angry circles" all day long. She could have calzone for lunch instead (p. 105).

Tree Pose

B.K.S. Iyengar (2002) writes that in any yoga pose, two things are required: *sense of direction* and *center of gravity*. Balance in this regard is the midpoint between resistance and surrender, the state in which firmness and suppleness unite. One of the classic poses, hence, is *Vrksasana* or "Tree Pose." It epitomizes a large, healthy tree rooted in the solidity of the earth and expanding toward the freedom of the sky. The tree can withstand gale force winds and driving storm, because its trunk is straight, roots are widespread, and branches accommodating. An immature tree with shallow roots, however, would be yanked from the earth.

A curious aspect of trees — they grow in two *opposite* directions — is edifying for our own personal development. A root-bound tree inevitably rots as it more and more tightens around itself, strangling out its sources of nutrients. We also mentally and spiritually decay as we cease to enlarge our foundational values and beliefs. Like a tree rooting itself deep in the soil while simultaneously flourishing in the radiant sky, we need to live our lives poised between resolve and openness. We must act out from our strengths *and* ascend to new ones. There is a pull downward and push upward as risk-taking is balanced by an ever growing embedding in principles. Over-stretching shifts the center of gravity, but the weakest part then becomes the point of remediation. In the jutting diagonals and tumult of life, balancing and rebalancing are the reoccurring themes of self-growth.

Health and morality

The clarion for balance in life is pronounced in the interwoven care of body and mind. The physical and mental are *interdependent* facets of our existence. Depletion of one limits the other; strengthening of one fortifies the other. In "comprehensive medicine," there are, as a result, five vital signs of wellbeing: blood pressure, temperature, respiration rate, pulse, and *pain*. The stabs and throbs of pain impinge upon the psychological, social, and vocational aspects of our lives, leading to depression, interfering with friendships, and disrupting work. Pain management is, accordingly, therapy that meets the coping needs of both the physical *and* emotional health of patients.

Morita (1928/1998) therein reproached those physicians who only treated the physical manifestation or organic genesis of an ailment. Any medical illness has some psychological component. Anyone who becomes diseased becomes, at least temporarily, *shinkeishitsu*. In consort, psychological difficulties are often manifested in physical symptoms and complaints. Morita therapy is thus an "integrative therapy in that the psyche and soma are naturally rebalanced and the natural healing power is enhanced" (Nakamura, u.d., p. 5). Therapeutic effects on psychophysiological and biochemical conditions, for example, including sleep and heart rate, have been found in patients undergoing treatment (Kitanishi & Mori, 1995).

Personal wellbeing, nevertheless, is built on more than our physical vitality and mental contentment. The Taoist doctor in the Chinese medical system is primarily a *sifu* ("teacher"), instructing patients about physical health, including preventative diet and exercise, but also how to become a more upstanding person. Salubrious morality and social centering bring individual health and inner peace into equilibrium with public health and world peace.

Hara

The robustness, agility, and stamina of our physical capabilities and movements are all dependent upon the condition of our *hara*. We cannot jump, jaunt, stoop, twist, walk, lift, bend, or chant without its core involvement (Yamaoka, 1976, pp. 15-16). The *hara*, however, is more than the center of gravity for physical balance and health. It is also where we optimally filter our interactions with the outer world and resolve our tensions and problems. If we listen, speak, counsel, clear our minds, and settle our emotions through the *hara*, we will not overreact from stress, grow wildly impatient, spin out of control, or explode in anger. Everything "digested" through the *hara* neutralizes the improvident response and overbearing will (Yamaoka, 1976, p. 37).

The antithesis of *hara* is what astrophysicists term "dark energy." This mysterious inverse of gravity does not emit gainful light and pulls things apart. It is the gloomy mass that we cannot see or draw upon. Dark energy is analogous to the fragmentation and emptiness of "off-balance" lives, ones not settled or focused enough to bring others closer and dearer. The Japanese thus refer to the *hara* as the symbol of integration and integrity. We propagate the *hara* in order to approach life with a balanced perspective, thoughtful manner, and measured conduct. Our up-front actions will then be in accord with our *sei no yokubo* (Matesz, 1990, p. 22).

Merging Currents: Through moderation and integrity we are brought nearer to others and the world.

Chapter 11

Morita Life Principle Eleven
Oneness

"Life flows from being intimate"

I wonder if satori *(enlightenment) means to break through such confusion and become one with the present reality, to go beyond verbal processing— where the external environment, the ego, objectivity and subjectivity, and emotion and knowledge all become one and free of incongruities.*

Shoma Morita
(1928/1998, p. 4)

Quietly floating duck

A number of Japanese scholars have related Morita's view of psychopathology to Buddhism, citing in particular his frequent use of Zen sayings and proverbs (Kitanishi & Mori, 1995, p. 248). Although Morita was superbly knowledgeable about religions in general, he was more likely appropriating terms familiar to his clients and colleagues to describe his treatment theory. Morita-dō is *not* a religion but a lifeway that can be integrated into a spectrum of belief systems (Quanrun, 2004; Tro, 1993; Matesz, 1990). Morita was more physician than metaphysician, having graduated in 1902 from the Medical School of Tokyo Imperial University. He was basically concerned with *perceptible reality*: the world of observable phenomena. Fact is truth *(jujitsu tadashin)*. What we see, hear, and touch are sufficient for a worthy life. The inspiration and guidance to live already exist within ourselves *(sei no yokubo)* and the immediate tasks at hand.

Morita was not unmindful of the need for "awe" in our lives, but held that a spiritual life is to be "one with everyday reality" *(arugamama)*. We can always rely upon and, hence, submit ourselves to factual evidence (Usa, 1940; Morita, 1974). D. T. Suzuki, et al. (1963) parallel Morita's reprove of the "unnatural complication of a supernatural influence" by their anecdote of a duck quietly floating on the surface of the lake. The duck is not to be separated from its legs "most busily moving, though unseen, under the water." Dualists generally miss the "coherent whole in its concrete totality" (p. 65). Any influence of the supernatural can be witnessed in the natural. Spirituality is not as much *getting there* as it is *being here*. It is not the beckoning of an intangible higher level of existence (what Ram Dass calls the "appetite for other planes"), but tangible oneness with all corners and encounters of our daily lives. Menter (2002) thus implores us to open your eyes and we will be where we need to be. Prayers, chants, and pleadings are less for "summoning miracles" from some distant realm as much as "enabling dedication" to what is right before us (p. 105).

Onsen

Japan luxuriates in 10,000 thermal mineral springs *(onsen)*, more than any other country in the world. Its 600 active volcanoes are the restive source of these wellsprings that never freeze even when surrounding surface water is gripped in an icy and gray snare. They are the "brilliantly fluid core" of a magical life-force that never dries up and never stops (Palmer, 2006, p. 23). Most of the outdoor springs are near frothing streams and gorges framed by verdant mountains.

Associated with the *onsen* are hundreds of charming *ryokans* ("inns") that dot the countryside. One of Japan's ancient spiritual traditions is to journey to *ryokans* to regenerate and purify in the barely tolerable hot water (131-158 degrees Fahrenheit). The aim is not so much to be clean from grime but to cleanse oneself, meditate, and heal (Draper, 2006). Waters rich in calcium, magnesium, and other minerals are said to be good for relieving bronchitis, gastrointestinal aliments, arthritis, circulatory problems, eczema, stress, and anxiety (Van Itallie & Hadley, 2000).

After washing several times prior to entering the communal bath (*sento*), patrons sidle into the genial waters. Others are kind enough not to stare (too much), but bathing is still a social event inasmuch as bathers enter into *hadaka no tsukiai* ("naked relationship"). Most *sento*, however, are now separated by gender because of the mores imposed on the Japanese culture by the postwar Western occupiers. Sitting silent in the steaming waters, patrons restfully rejuvenate, immerse in the idyllic surroundings, and draw in the mountain air. Removed from the frenzy of city life and hectic work schedules, the Japanese bask in the "greater spirituality" of reconnecting with nature's quietude, their sybaritic selves, and polite others.

Shinkeishitsu

Our identity is in our experiences: we are indistinguishable from the confluence of events in our lives. What we experience makes up who we are. Neurotic persons, however, separate themselves from their very own experiences, perceiving these as threats to their wellbeing. They become further removed from living as they wallow in self-loathing. *Shinkeishitsu*, as described by Morita (1928/1998), is the torment of "alienation from self" and "estrangement from others." Both are wrought by phobias, high anxiety, and overperfectionism.

In the acclaimed Sofia Coppola film, *Lost in Translation*, an aging, disconsolate American actor, Bob Harris, reluctantly travels to Tokyo to be the showpiece of a Japanese whiskey commercial. Bob is "lost" in Japan. He is unable to decipher the "odd mannerisms" of the Japanese populace, cannot speak their "gibberish," and misinterprets their (mis)pronunciation of English words. A female escort, for example, sent to his room by his Japanese hosts, badgers him to "*R*ip my stockings!" Bob haplessly hears it as "*L*ip my stockings!" Not knowing what to do, he infuriates the woman.

Bob sits listlessly for hours in the hermetic hotel bar, nonplussed to the vibrant clatter of the world's most populous city and indifferent to the rich urban museum of Japan's cultural icons. He is also adrift in his career and marriage, sleepwalking in the apathetic glow of depression and demise. At the same plush hotel is another American, a young wife left to herself by her ambitious photographer husband, who has scurried away to another country on assignment. Charlotte is also dolefully "off course." Her once youthful passion for life and marriage has been subdued by her husband's callous inattention to her needs. With little else to do, Charlotte restlessly wanders through the sights and sounds of Tokyo or smokes broodingly in the hotel bar. She furtively "waits" for something (someone?).

The premise of this uncomplicated film is "everyone wants to be found." About the time we feel utterly lost and alone, some unanticipated and stunning connection occurs. An improbable and sweet love develops between Bob and Charlotte. He is spellbound by her refreshing simplicity and quiet attentiveness. She is drawn to his undemanding responsiveness and mature caring. This is a romance with discrete kisses and unbeknownst consummation. It is a pairing of souls *not* lost in the "translation of intimacy" across generation and circumstance.

In *all* stages of life, a sense of belonging sets the scenery and props for living well. Albom (1997) reminds us that when we try to substitute material things for love, or for gentleness or for tenderness, or for a sense of comradeship, it never really works for property "does not hug back" (p. 125). Living well comes from bridging *dis*connection. We are most spirited and alive when we feel connected to matters and persons beyond our private fears and troubles. Humans need the interplay of others. As Corey (2008) writes, "We have a desire for intimacy, a hope to be significant in another's world, and a desire to feel that another's presence is important in our world" (p. 231).

Mori, as in "Mori-ta," coincidentally means "forest." Trees shield other trees; stalwart growth occurs in groves. Even the Japanese pine planted in a pot and cultivated in miniature (bonsai) is meant to symbolize a great forest. Bonsai trees, moreover, require as many as fifty years to take form. This is an art peculiar to the Japanese — perhaps because it depends upon a family system under which successive generations are willing to devote the same care to a plant over many decades (Narazaki, 1970, p. 11).

Re-spect

The Japanese are a culture of *amae*, which means to presume upon another's love or indulgence. It is epitomized in the mother's unconditional love for her children: caring for them with generosity and kindness without regard to inconvenience or hardship. This spirit of "trustful dependence" was fostered in the *mura* ("village") where a sense of belonging and community order were paramount. Villagers could depend upon one another without fear of being cheated or disadvantaged in any way (Lafayette De Mente, 1997, p. 8). The related Japanese value of *wa* has two aspects: the respect for the rights of others and the willingness to set aside individual wishes when they conflict with the common interests of the group (Gudykunst & Nishida, 1994). Harmony is achieved through conformance and consensus. The Japanese abhor being conspicuous and are reluctant to air opinions. They will do the topmost to reach agreement and preserve the network of multi-faceted associations.

The Japanese, despite being touted for this group orientation, have been historically notorious for having little or no sympathy for "strangers." Entanglements of any kind with *tanin* ("outsiders") are regarded with suspicion and are to be avoided. *Tanin* are sly competitors at best and ruthless enemies at worst (Lafayette De Mente, 1997, p. 358). Although *tanin* are often non-Japanese, there are also Japanese who are not admitted to the mainstream of society. These *burakumin* ("new commoners") are outcasts who are racially and ethnically no different than other Japanese. Yet, the traditional identification of the *burakumin* with occupations associated with the impurities of death and slaughter—butchering and tanning—has made them "untouchables." Parents forbid their children to marry someone from this group. Today's estimated 3 million *burakumin* also face employment and housing discrimination. As Albom (1997, p. 154) remarks, when we are threatened, we start to only look out for ourselves.

Respect, on the other hand, literally means to "look again" at the nuances of another person's hopes, concerns, and way of thinking. Everyone we encounter in life may or may not deserve our return of respect, but most probably deserve more than our oversimplifications, biases, and defenses. Elie Wiesel (1996), the Nobel Peace Prize recipient and Holocaust survivor, has cogently noted that hatred is always seeing someone as "the other." The stranger is the one we unashamedly disdain as not having the same humanity as we do. *Their* feelings, sensibilities, and yearnings are hardly comparable to ours. It is unproblematic to commit cruelty, violence, or war against those with whom we feel *un*connected. Ruland (1999) therefore writes that true empathy means that we must focus, not on group abstractions — such as everyone poor, feminine, old, Hindu, or victimized, all to be loved or hated in a global hazy prejudgment — but on one distinct person at a time. Then we are more likely to uncover "a saga of human dreams and misery not unlike our own" (p. 31).

Elongation

Scaravelli (1991) teaches that the essence of yoga practice is to elongate and extend rather than pull and push. We are, for example, shorter by three-quarters of an inch at the end of the working day than in the morning because of the compression of cartilage in the spine. Resting in horizontal position or executing spinal lengthening relieves this unhealthful pressure. The parallel to life is that we must proffer our life energy to others rather than contract it for purely selfish ends. The word yoga, indeed, comes from the ancient Sanskrit word "yoke." The individual self does not vanish in this union as much as it is found.

According to Morita (Tanishima, 1973), the "confined self" is self-preoccupation leading to neurosis. The "extended self" is sensitivity to the needs of others leading to service. In Morita's original residential treatment, for example, a family-like atmosphere existed: Morita's wife was *haha* ("mother") and Morita was *chichi* ("father") to the patients (Ushijima, 2004). Patients also supported and influenced one another. Morita therapy is thus said to be the first group psychotherapy to be practiced in Japan (Kitanishi & Mori, 1995, p. 246). This tradition has continued in some settings, including Kyoto's Sansei Hospital. As described by Benhamou

(2004), there is a strong relationship between the Morita patient and the psychiatrist, almost a respectful paternal-like relationship. The patient is also progressively socialized to the group of patients, and becomes an intimate member of the entire therapeutic community.

We live most powerfully as we become devoted to helping one another. When the Dalai Lama was asked about his religion, he said, "My religion is kindness." When we truly engage others in kindness, we ourselves become whole. Offensive conduct, unbridled pride, or self-serving avarice affects our spiritual wellbeing because it causes rifts with others. The root of the word "heal," in fact, is "to make whole, to bring together." As Ornish (2004) counsels, anything that promotes isolation leads to chronic stress and, in turn, may lead to illnesses like heart disease and cancer as well as premature death. Anything, in contrast, that promotes a sense of intimacy, community, and connection can be healing.

Yin/Yang

Watts (1961) elucidates the Taoist symbol of Yin/Yang, the black and white fishes in eternal intercourse, as everything fitting into place in an indescribable harmony. Yin/Yang is not the "marriage of opposites" as much as the revelation that there is nothing wantonly mistreated, foolishly forgotten, relegated to the outside, or left behind. Pachuta (1989) alike says that to the Western mind, things are black *and* white or black *or* white, but in the Eastern way, things are black/white. The inseparable Yin and Yang gently wrestle with each other because nothing in the universe is one or the other. Everything contains Yin/Yang. They are part of the same reality. Yin/Yang, moreover, is not only outside of us in the universe but also within us because we are part of the universe (p. 70).

Nowhere is this oneness more disclosed than the inextricable human bond with water. Water occupies 70% of the earth's surface-yet we have no gills! It makes up 60% of our bodies-yet we must rehydrate each day! Land and sea, body and fluid are the planetary and personal Yin/Yang. Water has this inimitable quality to *hold together* both our earthly and corporeal habitation. From Beijing to Chicago and Bangkok to Rio de Janeiro the skies share moisture that is part of one vast system that circumnavigates the earth (Wood, 2003, p. 301). This interconnectedness, as Palmer (2006) describes, is even more sophisticated:

> [The river] reminds us that we are connected, not just to water, but everywhere water has been and everywhere it is going. Beyond that, we are connected not only to one river, but to all of them. We are part of the hydrologic cycle. The rivers, afterall, flow in our veins.
>
> (p. 213)

Transboundary waters capture the nature and significance of ubiquitous water. Namibia's Orange River, for example, seamed by craggy mountains and insipid dunes, undulates through Botswana and skirts the northern border of South Africa to the Atlantic Ocean. The uniqueness of the Orange is not only the geopolitical boundaries it demarcates but its dispersal of generous traces of diamonds along its course. Over millions of years the river has sluiced diamonds from basins deep in the mid-African continent to be deposited at its rivermouth and transported by currents along the deserted shoreline. Uppermost cooperation between impacted nations and heavily enforced restricted zones ban those who would scour the river and outlet for this coveted gemstone. These are not the "conflict diamonds" that have subsidized the bloody civil warfare in bordering Angola and Sierra Leone, and whose international trade has been condemned by the United Nations. Those black market diamonds are linked to fearsome atrocities and death. Still, in the dire circumstance of the mounting pan-African water crisis, what is *most* indispensable: glittering ornaments or life itself?

Riparian nations must continually solve the equitable use of fresh water resources that cross jurisdictional borders, including those flowing beneath or underlying the surface (Campana, 2005). Appreciable increases in the human population—at present 6.5 billion—are expected to continue in the coming decades. Additional water will be required for nonfungible (nonexchangeable) uses such as irrigated agriculture, livestock watering, domestic supply, and ecosystem support. Today, 1.1 billion people are without access to potable drinking water. The distribution of water is not uniform, nor is it correlated well with population densities (Wood, 2003, p. 301). The Amazon for example, is the largest river in the world (in terms of volume and water cubic meters/second). It accounts for 15% of the global runoff but its basin contains only 0.5% of the world's population. China has 21% of the world's population but only 7% of the global runoff. We must doubtlessly be more liberal and unequivocal in our water sharing.

Homo delphinus

The breath-hold sport of free-diving is a perfect meeting of human and environment. The late Jacques Mayol (1927-2001), known as *homo delphinus* ("dolphin man") was the pioneer waterman who, in 1976, was the first to dive below 100 meters (330 feet) without the assistance of air tanks (Mayol, 2000). Mayol was a Frenchman who was born in Shanghai and raised in Japan. His life desire was to rejoin our aquatic past and become one with nature. A dolphin named Clown at the Seaquarium in Miami, Florida was said to have taught Mayol how to hold his breath longer on each dive, how to behave underwater, and how to totally integrate with the ocean. Mayol improved these dive skills with the practice of yoga and Eastern philosophies.

The current world-record holder, Pipin Ferreras of Florida, has descended, aided by an 80-pound gravity-sled ("no-limits diving"), to 532.8 feet. This is the depth at which nuclear submarines operate! Ferreras has commented that his true happiness is the deep water, a place that has dared him to hold his breath for up to 7.5 minutes, and where his lungs shrink to the size of oranges. Despite his incredible physiological attainments, Ferreras submits that the mind is 100% of the difference in achieving great dives. The mind must be in a total *non-adversarial* relationship with the body. As his bodily functions power down to stillness and his mind quiets to a murmur, Ferreras defies irreversible brain damage from oxygen starvation (Tauber & Trischitta, 2000). Free-divers are astounding in their prowess and concentration as they plunge into the liquid abyss. They do not contest the water as troublesome foe, but enter its depths as encircling womb.

Merging Currents: Increasing wholeness and oneness are emulated by a profound gratefulness for life.

Chapter 12

Morita Life Principle Twelve Peace

"Life flows from being grateful"

Therapy is not based on those principles that encourage momentary happiness or superficial pleasure . . . To make an effort is to move toward true contentment.

Shoma Morita
(1928/1998, p. 96)

Saints and poets, maybe

In Thornton Wilder's magnificent play, "Our Town," the lead character, Emily, soon after her death, is allowed to observe her family members going about their daily routines. Finally, when she is ready to go to her grave, she sobs, "Do any human beings ever realize life while they live it? Every, every minute?" Emily hears only this smidgeon of assurance: "The saints and poets, maybe—they do some" (Mouw, 2004, p. 2). A contemporary rendering of this musing is *American Beauty*, the 1999 Academy Award film about the domestic wasteland of suburbia. The protagonist, Lester Burnham, is the crestfallen husband of an unfaithful wife and father to a sullen teenager. In the clutches of mid-life angst, Lester becomes smitten with a coquettish high school cheerleader, who reignites his lust for life. He charges into salvaging his drooping physique; resigns from his boorish job; and renounces meekness to his wife's mania and daughter's insolence.

A bleak "comedy" about an exceedingly dysfunctional family, the film interweaves Lester's looming confrontation with an abrasive, moralistic neighbor, the father of Lester's daughter's boyfriend. One evening, this fitful neighbor shoots Lester to remove the misconstrued menace to his son's "manhood" (and object of his own closeted erotic conflict). As Lester lies mortally wounded, events of his life flutter through his dimming mind. In spite of all the "craziness" and "miscues" in his life, Lester has arrived at an unfamiliar peace within himself. His final utterance is imparted with a smirk: "I feel gratitude for every moment of my stupid little life."

Kabat-Zinn (1994) laments when sublime clarity of life coincides with the explicit moment of death. It betrays that we have lived on a "fog-enshrouded, slippery slope right into our graves" (pp. xvi-xvii). Appreciation for life should be more than patches of sentiment, balm for the wounds of living, or benediction to slip into death. Demarest (2000) describes gratitude as "worship" (an easier pronunciation than the original "worth-ship" in the English language!). We have found that which is of matchless worth to us and worthy of our best. We are, in effect, unraveled from the full-blown narcissism that is sooner or later "antagonistic" to experiencing contentment (Reynolds, 1989, p. 188). Happiness is found not through self-gratification but through creating happiness for others (cf. Keller, 1933). This is what D. T. Suzuki (Ives, 1992) recommended as "secret virtue." We practice goodness without any thought of reward or recognition by others. The best giving, like the best action generally, is when there is no sense that it is a gift (Loy, 1985, p. 80).

Ralph Abernathy (1991) poignantly writes that the cemetery for his dear friend and slain civil rights leader, Martin Luther King, Jr., is "too small for his spirit" and the grave "too narrow for his soul." There is "no coffin, no crypt, and no stone that can hold his greatness" (p. 484). King's life was beset with insults, threats, and beatings until his assassination in Memphis on April 4, 1968. His storied and selfless path included periods when he did not always *feel* thankful and joyful. He was at times harried, despairing, and conflicted. His unflagging character, however, rested in the candor of his cause. His life was a calling that he would neither give up nor from which he could escape. This is the fealty of "builders," those who construct a better life for others as they do what matters most to them (Porras, Emery, & Thompson, 2006).

The Japanese laud persistence in the white heat of misfortune. Like the intrepid *koi*, classically presented in Hokusai's painting, *Carp in the Waterfall*, we are to scale the blitzing falls and transfigure into venerable dragons. This inspiring ardor was formalized in the Japanese warrior code of Bushido. The samurai were altogether trustworthy because they were not vested in material riches and had no fear of death. Their supreme loyalty was to their feudal overlord and Emperor. This code, in tempered form, continues today in Japan even though the last samurai, Saigo Takamori, died in 1877 while leading the ill-fated Satsuma revolt opposing westernization. Personal survival and success are less important than honorable and principled service.

360 sauces

A former colleague of mine groused that mealtime is a chore and a bore. The mission of his once-a-month shopping was to purchase a pallet of frozen meals. His dinners consisted of indiscriminately plucking out whatever was on top of his freezer stash, removing it from the carton, placing the tray in the microwave, zapping it, inhaling the tasteless morsels, and then summarily trashing the container. Any further exertion was tantamount to "squandering" his time. As Fujita (personal communication, October 20, 2004) remarks, since modern society pursues convenience and ease in food, it is not surprising that we have less tolerance for stress and have difficulty facing and acting upon any of the other exigencies of life. Talleyrand (1754-1838), the consummate French diplomat and gourmand, also said (undiplomatically), "France has three religions and 360 sauces but England has only three sauces and 360 religions!"

Gastronomes herald the entwining of food and pleasure, believing that the person who pays attention to the details of cooking is more likely to be indulgent in other details of life. Thoughtfulness about food interposes thoughtfulness in relationships, work, and other responsibilities. Food is vis vitalis! The alchemy of food and life was also a mainstay for my father. He was for most of his career the executive chef at a stellar French restaurant in Los Angeles. His prior toil as a migrant farm worker and grocery store proprietor had laid the foundation for his conspicuous career in traditional Provencal cooking. My father had two seasonings of wisdom related to food and life: "Japanese eat with their eyes" and "We approach food in the way we approach life."

Tsutsumu

The first of my father's adages conveys the importance of *how* a meal is offered to family, guests, or customers. The Japanese orchestrate food colors, shapes, and portions with tableware and service, because we *visually* welcome food before it touches our lips. The meal is to be pleasing in *all* aspects since it represented the preparer's estimation of the partakers. Haphazard or slipshod presentation intimates contempt, resentment, or apathy.

On the morning of a Kochi-ken (United States residents from the Kochi prefecture in Japan) picnic, my mother would awaken early to steam rice. After the rice was measured, washed, and cooked, it was gently fluffed and seasoned. Each grain was treated like a luminescent white pearl! My mother then hand-shaped dozens of triangular *musubi*, and flawlessly arranged them in neat rows in a *ju-bako* ("lacquered box"). When the box was filled, she would *tsutsumu* ("enwrap") it within a silk *furoshiki* ("wrapping cloth"). When we arrived at the picnic grounds, my mother would unroll a large straw mat and position the food she had prepared, including the "pampered" *musubi*. Each container would be meticulously placed according to size and contents. The mat was transformed into a canvas of Japanese food art!

As a child, I was puzzled by meticulousness that my mother brought to something as ordinary as *musubi* for an outdoor picnic. Why not hurriedly clump handfuls of rice together, and stuff the (misshapen) *musubi* into a plain brown paper bag? At the picnic, we could prosaically unfurl a tattered blanket (with decomposed leaves and blades of grass still clinging from the last picnic!); strew plastic grub tubs helter-skelter; disembowel the bag of *musubi*; and swoop into voracious consumption. Later in life, I realized that my mother was being delicately purposeful. It was one of the many ways that she practiced sensitivity toward family and relatives as well as old and new friends. She offered in her life and food the best she was able to. Food *is* communication.

Interpersonal relationships are identically built upon substance and conveyance. Accrued knowledge, legendary perspicuity, and preternatural experiences are corrupted if the sharing of these is marked with derision, scorn, or hubris. Is our delivery enfolded in linen or burlap? In Japanese custom, everything is discretely carried in *furashiki*: from tools to lunch and from martial arts ranking belts to gifts. It is considered ill-mannered to boast about achievements, flaunt one's possessions, or nettle envy or suspicion. Being superior or senior in status, attainments, or assets begs modesty more than swagger. We must exercise humility in order to prevent humiliating others.

Food and character

The second of my father's adages ("We approach food in the way we approach life") underscores that our character is detected and developed in our treatment of food. An old priest was diligently preparing a meal for his fellowship. The priest was asked why he concentrated so intently on such tasks instead of busily seeking enlightenment. His reply: "Cooking is useful to monks in disciplining themselves. Being able to cook a good meal *is* enlightenment. Concentrating completely on preparing a single dish eliminates my delusions" (Hirai, 1989, p. 17).

> ZEN STUDENT: So, Master, is the soul immortal or not? Do we survive our bodily death or do we get annihilated? Do we really reincarnate? Does our soul split up into component parts which get recycled, or do we as a single unit enter the body of a biological organism? And do we retain our memories or not?
>
> MASTER: Your breakfast is getting cold.
>
> (Smullyan, 1977, p. 194)

Modern American culture tends to be ambivalent about food. We have relegated convivial family dinners to nostalgic Norman Rockwell paintings. In their place we have proliferated drive-through gimmick restaurants serving bulk-processed trans-fatty chow, gobbled down unconsciously. Contemporaneously, we have hallowed an epicurean bill of fare concocted by superstar chefs, bon vivant restaurateurs, and boutique growers. We now have scintillating television food networks and celebrity cookbooks to inculcate new generations, because home menus scarcely ever consist of our own grandmother's (*obachan's*) favorite recipe.

Ornish (2000) alerts that when we rush through meals, we are likely to rush through life. When we feel nourished by food, we allow ourselves to feel nourished in other ways. When we choose to eat life-affirming foods, we choose to affirm our lives in other areas. That is, when we practice eating with attentiveness and appreciation, we are more likely to live in the same way. Virtually all cultures, for example, have some form of supplication before meals. The Japanese customarily nod, clasp their hands, and amiably enunciate, "*Itadakimasu,*" an acknowledgment for all the kindness that went into preparing the meal. At the meal's conclusion, "*Gochisosamadesu*" is conferred, a benediction of indebtedness. *Gochisō* is "delicacy." We appreciate the delicacies of healthful food and cordial relationships. In this context, meditation plumps the awareness of eating and eating with awareness becomes a meditation on life.

Tenzo

The belief that both the preparation and partaking of food constitute spiritual practice is at the heart of Soto Zen. Ruyak (1996) explains how *shojin ryori*, the vegetarian food of Japanese Zen temples, is for the body *and* spirit. The *tenzo* (priest responsible for preparing meals) takes great care in deciding upon the menu, procuring the ingredients, cooking, and serving the meal. The *tenzo* is to (1) *diversify* (combine fresh elements in a variety of ways and cook with more kinds of vegetables); (2) *improvise* (use imagination and recycle leftovers); and (3) *be attentive* (exercise thoughtfulness). What matters, however, more than the quality of the food or its nutritional balance, is the endowment of gratitude. While eating, the monks meditate on the life that has been given up so that they may live. Meals are partaken not impassively but in contrition. Before eating, a five-part meditation (*Gokan No Ge*) is reverentially chanted:

❖ We give thanks for the food about to be eaten and for the work that went into growing and making it.

❖ We reflect on whether our practice is worthy of all the sacrifice entailed in the meal.

❖ We vow to eat without complaint, greed, or covetousness.

❖ We bear in mind that food is medicine for health and wellbeing.

❖ We resolve gratefully to eat in order to work for the sake of all sentient beings.

Perfection in an average day

Brad Herzog (1999) describes an 11-month, cross-country trip with his photographer wife, Amy, as travel prompted by the sense of being closed in by their careers and being part of the stampede to "make a living instead of a life." Herzog, a disillusioned Gen X-er, confesses that he found himself sitting in front of a computer terminal 10 hours a day, a chronicler of the world whose own world was limited to a back room with a view of an icy parking lot (p. 96). Uprooting themselves from their Chicago apartment, the Herzogs put a down payment on a 34-foot motor home and began their 21,000-mile roadtrip. They mulled over what "states of mind" they would discover in the residents they would encounter. They visited towns with names like Pride (Alabama), Faith (South Dakota), Wisdom (Montana), and Inspiration (Arizona).

One of the last stops the Herzogs made was the Illinois village of Joy, a dozen or so blocks surrounded by a sea of crops. Even amidst all the soybeans and corn, Joy is no longer a thriving farm town; it is a bedroom community of a mere 450 residents. The Herzogs uncovered nothing extraordinarily joyful in Joy. Even as an unassuming place, however, the town revealed something unforeseen *and* comforting: the wanderlust to be "elsewhere" might culminate in the gratification of "coming back." The glories sought on the open road, and some other place to be, are often on the street where we already live.

Life is not as much a longing as it is a benefit (Smullyan, 1977, pp. ix, xi), but in the pursuit of happiness, we have forgotten to be happy. When we arrive at finding perfection in an average day (cf. Albom, 1997, p. 176), we have progressed to the "punctum" of our lives, the spot where we know we are privileged. This gratitude revives us to return full circle to the threshold principle of "attention." As Smullyan (1977) reasons, a "purely passive serenity is kind of dull, and an anxiety-ridden awareness is not very appealing" (p. xi). The soul mates of mindfulness *and* appreciation lift us to the sans pareil watermark of life.

Merging Currents: The flow of being observant, purposeful, natural, present, realistic, intuitive, for-giving, emotion-all, response-able, centered, intimate, and grateful carries us on an amazing life course!

Epilogue

*When we look at mountains with a
smile, the mountains smile back; when
we look at water through our tears,
the water also cries.*

Shoma Morita
(1928/1998, p. 79)

Nestled between the crown of the contiguous United States, Mount Whitney, and the nethermost Death Valley, is the site of my ignoble birthplace: Manzanar ("apple orchard", Sp.). Manzanar was set on federal lands parceled from the Northern Paiute Nation. It was an arid bastion of barbed wire perimeters, austere rows of hastily constructed tarpaper barracks, and menacing sentry posts that interned 10,000 Japanese Americans throughout the duration of World War II. There was scant of a natural river to live by in this dust-storm wasteland of many tears and few smiles.

Today, through this sparse area, the Los Angeles Aqueduct labors for hundreds of trenched miles to provide 70% of that city's water supply. The Owens Valley itself is mostly parched flats and rutted foothills, which produce acrid particulate air pollution due to its location in the wind-swept high dessert. It is the bountiful snowmelt from the Eastern Sierra Nevada Mountains and diversion from ample lakes to the north that have allowed the nation's largest megatropolis to quench its staggering demands for water. Millions of lives desperately depend upon this colossal movement of water; they drink deeply from this mighty source.

Whether it is machine-carved channels or virgin woodland creeks, the marvel of coalescing tributaries or floodplain of teeming deltas, waterways are grantors of life. Across the panorama of our personal lives, we must also find an unfailing river to live by: one whose undaunted flow carries us far and well, and whose purity inoculates us against mean realities. The energy of this river must reliably wash away the quagmire of vagueness about how to live, and free the silt of our woes to follow that meaningful course. At first, we are the fallen autumn leaf of the Japanese maple, floating lithe on mere traces of the downstream current. We sense the subtle drift but are tentative about the destination. In due course, we find resonance with the currents and become the powerful river itself . . .

References

AARP. (2004, September/October). Nelson Mandela's lesson. *AARP The Magazine*, 72.

Abernathy, R. (1991). *And the walls came tumbling down*. New York: Harper Collins.

Albom, M. (1997). *Tuesdays with Morrie*. New York: Doubleday.

Azuma, N. (2004). A study of the relationship between the origin of Morita Therapy and Montessori Educational Method. *Journal of Morita Therapy*, *15* (1), 69.

Azuma, N. (2001). *Goals of Morita therapy: Mobilizing clients beyond anxious hesitation*. Paper presented at the 20th International Human Science Research Conference, Tokyo, Japan, August 19-22, 2001.

Bagnold, E. (1935). *National Velvet*. New York: Avon Books.

Baker, N. (2003). *A box of matches*. New York: Random House.

Banks, S. (1983). *Second chance*. Wauwatosa, WI: Pine Mountain Press.

Belsky, J. (2007). *Experiencing the lifespan*. New York: Worth Publishers.

Benhamou, H. (2004, October 18). *The Sansei and Daisan hospitals: Two models of Morita therapy. A psychoanalytic point of view*. Lecture presented at the Fifth International Meeting for Morita Therapy, Shanghai, China.

Blatner, A. (2000). *Foundations of psychodrama: History, theory, and practice* (4th ed.). New York: Springer.

Buford, B. (2004). *Finishing well: What people who really live do*. Brentwood, TN: Integrity Publishers.

Byrne, R. (2006). *The secret*. New York: Atria/Beyond Words.

Callahan, G. N. (1998). *River odyssey: A story of the Colorado Plateau*. Niwot, CO: University Press of Colorado.

Callenbach, E. (2000). *Living cheaply with style* (2nd ed). Berkeley, CA: Ronin.

Campana, M. E. (2005, September/October). Foreword: Transboundary ground water. *Ground Water, 43*(5), 646.

Carlin, P. A. and Fowler, J. (1999, July 26). Light on her feet. *People Magazine*, pp. 79-80.

Cather, W. (1997). *El Dorado: A Kansas recessional*. Charlottesville: University of Virginia.

Chapman, R. A. (Ed.). (2006). *The clinical use of hypnosis in cognitive behavioral therapy: A practitioner's casebook*. New York: Springer.

Char, T. (1970). *Chinese proverbs with bilingual text*. San Francisco: Jade Mountain Press.

Charlesworth, J. R. and Jackson, M. (2004). Solution-focused brief counseling: An approach for professional school counselors. In B. T. Erford (Ed.), *Professional school counseling: A handbook of theories, programs & practices* (pp. 139-148). Austin, TX: CAPS Press.

Christians In-Depth Fellowship. (1978, June). *CID Newsletter, 7*.

Clinton, B. (2004). *My life*. New York: Alfred A. Knopf.

Cobb, J. (1975). *Christ in a pluralistic age*. Philadelphia: Westminster.

Corey, J. (2008). *Theory and practice of group counseling* (7th ed.). Belmont, CA: Thomson Brooks/Cole.

Covey, S. (2000). *Living the 7 habits: The courage to change*. New York: Free Press.

Csikszentmihalyi, M. (1990). *Flow: The psychology of optimal experience*. New York: Harper and Row.

Cui, Y. (2004, October 18). *Application and study of Morita therapy*. Lecture presented at the Fifth International Meeting for Morita Therapy, Shanghai, China.

Davidson, R. J. (2003, September). Affective neuroscience and psychophysiology: Toward a synthesis. *Psychophysiology, 40*(5). 655-665.

Davidson, R. J. (2000). Cognitive neuroscience needs affective neuroscience (and vice versa). *Brain and Cognition, 42*, 89-92.

Davidson, R. J., Kabat-Zinn, J., Schumacher, J., Rosenkranz, M., Muller, D., Santorelli, S., Urbanowski, F., Harrington, A., Bonus, K., and Sheridan, J. F. (2003). Alterations in brain and immune function produced by mindfulness meditation. *Psychosomatic Medicine, 65,* 564-570.

Davis, J. (u.d.). *Morita therapy.* (Mimeographed).

Demarest, G. (2000, March). Simple and profound, gentle but firm. *Theology, News and Notes,* pp. 10-11.

DeMenthe, B. L. (1997). *Dictionary of Japanese cultural code words.* Chicago: National Textbook Company.

Dimidjian, S. and Linehan, M. M. ((2003). Mindfulness practice. In W. O'Donohue, J. E. Fisher, and S. C. Hayes (Eds.), *Cognitive behavior therapy: Applying empirically supported techniques in your practice* (pp. 229-237). Hoboken, NJ: Wiley.

Doi, T. (1977). *The anatomy of dependence.* Translated by Jon Bester. Tokyo: Kodansha.

Dowd, E. T. and Healy, J. M. (Eds.). (1986). *Case studies in hypnotherapy.* New York: The Guilford Press.

Draper, R. (2006, August 15). A cleansing experience. *American Way,* 774-885.

Easterbrook, G. (2004). *The progress paradox: How life gets better while people feel worse.* New York: Random House.

Ellis, A. (1996). *Better, deeper, and more enduring brief therapy: The rational emotive behavior therapy approach.* New York: Brunner/Mazel.

Fackler, M. (2007, February 15). Translating the Toyota way. *The New York Times,* pp. C1, C4.

Fox, M. (2002). *Lucky man: A memoir.* New York: Hyperion.

Fujita, C. (1990, October). On the meaning of *toraware* (being mentally captive and *sunao* (compliance) in Morita therapy. *Journal of Morita Therapy, 1*(2), 183-187.

Frager, R. (u.d.). The psychology of the samurai. *Psychology Today, 48,* 53, 68.

Frankl, V. (1959). *Man's search for meaning.* Boston: Beacon Press.

Frankl, V. (1955). *The doctor and the soul.* New York: Alfred A. Knopf.

Gleick, P. H. (1996). Water resources. In S. H. Schneider (Ed.), *Encyclopedia of climate and weather* (Vol. 2, pp. 817-823). New York: Oxford University Press.

Goleman, D. (1997). *Emotional intelligence.* New York: Bantam.

Goolsbee, A. (2007, March 1). Why do the richest people rarely intend to give it all away? *The New York Times,* p. C3.

Gross, A. (2000, August). Ram Dass: A Western guru finds peace while fighting to save his life. *Modern Maturity*, 12, 14, 16.

Gross, J. J. (2002). Emotion regulation: Affective, cognitive, and social consequences. *Psychophysiology*, *39*, 281-291.

Gudykunst, W. B. and Nishida, T. (1994). *Bridging North American/ Japanese differences*. Thousand Oaks, CA: Sage.

Hammond, H. and Ferguson, G. (1998, July/August). The time of your life. *Yoga Journal*, 72, 73-79.

Han, T. N. (u.d.) Retrieved April 16, 2004, from Vallecitos Mountain Refuge Web site: www.vallecitos.org/home.html

Harayda, J. (2004, March 15). My turn: He was spared once, but not a second time. *Newsweek*, 14.

Hasegawa, Y. (1993). *Daily calendar*. Tokyo: Seikatsu No Hakkenkai.

Hasegawa, Y. (1990, Spring). Hakkenkai's method of studying Morita theory: A group learning approach to overcoming neurosis. *International Bulletin of Morita Therapy*, 3(1), 26-34.

Heat-Moon, W. L. (2001). In Dancer, D. D., *The four seasons of Kansas*. Lawrence: University Press of Kansas.

Herendeen, W. H. (1986). *From landscape to literature*. Pittsburg: Duquesne University Press.

Herzog, B. (1999, July). Joy, Illinois. *Sky*, 96-101.

Hirai, T. (1989). *Zen meditation and psychotherapy*. Tokyo: Japan Publications.

Horney, K. (1952). The paucity of inner experiences. *International Journal of Psychoanalysis*, *12*(1), 3-9.

Hyams, J. (1979). *Zen in the martial arts*. New York: G.P. Putnam's Sons.

Ikuta, K. (1996). A consideration on the concept of health. *Japanese Journal of Public Health*, *43*(12), 1005-1008.

Ishiyama, I. (2004, October 18). *Integrated Morita-based counseling: A 3 phase intervention model developed in Canada*. Lecture presented at the Fifth International Meeting for Morita Therapy, Shanghai, China.

Ishiyama, I. (1990, Fall). Meaningful Life Therapy. *International Bulletin of Morita Therapy*, 3(2), 77-84.

Ishiyama, I. (1990, May/June). A Japanese perspective on client inaction: Removing attitudinal blocks through Morita therapy. *Journal of Counseling and Development*, *68*, 566-570.

Ishiyama, I. (1988). Morita therapy: A treatment of dogmatic self containment in anxious and nervous clients. *The Psychotherapy Patient, 4*(3/4), 243-262.

Ishiyama, I. (1987, June). Use of Morita therapy in shyness counseling in the West: Promoting clients' self-acceptance and action taking. *Journal of Counseling and Development, 65*, 547-551.

Itami, J. (2004, October 18). *Meaningful Life Therapy*. Paper presented at the Fifth International Meeting for Morita Therapy, Shanghai, China.

Itami, J. (1990). Application of Morita therapy for cancer and intractable disease. *Journal of Morita Therapy, 1*, 239-241.

Ives, C. (1992). *Zen awakening and society*. Honolulu: University of Hawaii Press.

Iyengar, B. K. S. (2002). *The tree of Yoga: Yoga of vrksa*. Boston: Shambhala.

James, W. (1890). *The principles of psychology*. Retrieved November 25, 2006, from Stanford University Web site: http://plato.stanford.edu/entries/james/

Japan Atlas. (2006). *The Shimanto River*. Retrieved September 2, 2006, from WebJapan: *http://web-japan.org/atals/nature/nat31.html*.

Jianlin, J. (2004, October 19). *Psychotherapy practice in China: How to integrate the Western therapeutic skills and the traditional Chinese culture for treatment of clients who suffer from psychological disorders*. Lecture presented at the Fifth International Meeting for Morita Therapy, Shanghai, China.

Jinsheng, L. (2004, October 17). *Training strategy based on Morita therapy for test anxiety: The unique intelligence of the Eastern philosophical Morita therapy*. Lecture presented at the Fifth International Meeting for Morita Therapy, Shanghai, China.

Joh, H. (1997). Disaster stress of the 1995 Kobe earthquake. *Japan Psychologia, 40*, 192-200.

Johnstone, B. (2005, January/February). After the quake, not before. *Far Eastern Economic Review, 168*(2), 78.

Joiner-Bey, H. (2002, Summer). Water . . . essential for athletes. *Healthsmart Today*, 62-64.

Jones, D. (2007, February 19). P&G CEO wields high expectations but no whip. *USA Today*, p. 3B.

Kabat-Zinn, J. (1994). *Wherever you go, there you are*. New York: Hyperion.

Kapleau, P. (1989). *Zen: Merging of East and West*. New York: Doubleday Anchor Books.

Kapleau, P. (1967). *The three pillars of Zen*. Boston: Beacon Press.

Karmarka, U. R. and Buonomano, D. V. (20007, February 1). Timing in the absence of clocks: Encoding time in neural network states. *Neuron, 53* (3), 427-438.

Kaufman, M. (1999, November 2). Emotions. *The Washington Post*, pp. 13, 15-17, 19.

Keene, D. (1989). The Japanese idea of beauty. *WQ, 128-135.

Keller, H. (1933, February). The simplest way to be happy. *Home Magazine*. Retrieved October 30, 2006, from American Foundation for the Blind Web site: http://*www.afb.org*

Keller, H. (1903/2003). *The story of my life*. Retrieved October 30, 2006, from American Foundation for the Blind Web site: http://*www.afb.org*/mylife/book.asp?ch=P1Ch4

Kelman, A. (2003). *A river and its city: The nature of landscape in New Orleans*. Berkeley: University of California Press.

Kennett, J. (1972). *Selling water by the river: A manual of Zen training*. New York: Random House.

Kirmayer, L. J. (2002, September). Psychopharmacology in a globalizing world: the use of antidepressants in Japan. *Transcultural Psychiatry, 39*(3), 295-322.

Kitanaka, J. (2003, June). Jungians and the rise of psychotherapy in Japan: A brief historical note. *Transcultural Psychiatry, 40*(2), 239-247.

Kitanishi, K. and Mori, A. (1995). Morita therapy: 1919 to 1995. *Psychiatry and Clinical Neurosciences, 49*, 245-254.

Koga, Y. (1967, April). On Morita therapy. *Jikeikai Medical Journal, 14*, 73-79.

Kondo, A. (1975). Morita therapy: Its socio-historical context. In Arieti, S. and Chrzanowski, G. (Eds.), *New dimensions in psychiatry: A world view*, pp. 239-59. New York: John Wiley & Sons.

Kora, T. (1990, Spring). An overview of the theory and practice of Morita therapy (Part 2). *International Bulletin of Morita Therapy, 3*(1), 7-13.

Kora, T. (1989, Fall). An overview of the theory and practice of Morita therapy. *International Bulletin of Morita Therapy, 2*(2), 70-79.

Kora, T. (1968). A method of instruction in psychotherapy. *Jikeikai Medical Journal, 15*, 312-325.

Kora, T. (1967, March). *Jibun wo shiru* (Know thyself). NHK reprint of radio broadcast.

Kora, T. (1965, October). Morita therapy. *International Journal of Psychiatry, 1*, 611-640.

Koren, L. (1994). *Wabi-sabi for artists, designers, poets, and philosophers.* Berkeley, CA: Stone Bridge.

Kusama, M. (1973). *Some concepts in Morita psychotherapy.* Oakland, CA: Christians In-Depth Fellowship, 1.

Lafayette De Mente, B. (1997). *NTC's dictionary of Japanese cultural code words.* Lincolnwood, IL: NTC Publishing Group.

Lee, B. (1975). *Tao of Jeet Kune Do.* Santa Clarita, CA: Ohara.

Levine, J. (2004, March-April). Uphill racer. *AARP, 42,* 43.

LeVine, P. (2004, October 17). *Silence during Morita therapy: Display of desire in those with trauma history.* Lecture presented at the Fifth International Meeting for Morita Therapy, Shanghai, China.

LeVine, P. (1994, November). Influence of Morita therapy on Karen Horney's final analysis. *Australian Psychologist, 29*(3), 153-157.

LeVine, P. (1993, September/October). Morita-based therapy and its use across cultures in the treatment of bulimia nervosa. *Journal of Counseling and Development, 72,* 82-90.

Lineen, J. (1999, March/April). Take me to the river. *Yoga Journal,* 64-71.

Lock, M. (1993). *Encounters with aging: Mythologies of menopause in Japan and North America.* Berkeley: University of California Press.

Loeb, P. R. (1999). *Soul of a citizen: Living with conviction in a cynical time.* New York: St. Martin's.

Loy, D. (1985, January). Wei-wu-wei: Non-dual action. *Philosophy East and West, 35*(1), 73-87.

Luc, V. and Gaudriault, C. (2005, August 1). Life after death. *Time, 166*(5), 40-43.

Maeda, F, and Nathan, J. H. (1999). Understanding *taijin kyofusho* through its treatment, Morita therapy. *Journal of Psychosomatic Research, 46*(6), 525-530.

Mashino, H. (2004, October 18). *Focus on Morita therapy as psychotherapy.* Lecture presented at the Fifth International Meeting for Morita Therapy, Shanghai, China.

Matesz, D. (1990, Spring). Morita and Buddhism: On the nature of suffering. *International Bulletin of Morita Therapy, 3*(1), 14-25.

Matsuda, Y. (2004, October 18). *Application of Morita therapy in an Australian context: Structural and theoretical implications for psychology curricula*. Lecture presented at the Fifth International Meeting for Morita Therapy, Shanghai, China.

Mayol. J. (2000). *Homo delphinus*. Reddick, FL: Idelson-Gnocchi.

McNutt, W. F. (1923, December). Vis medicatrix naturae. *California State Journal of Medicine, 21*(12), 510-511.

Menter, M. (2003, September/October). Chop wood, carry water. *Body and soul,* 100-102, 104-105.

Miller, S. D., Hubble, M. A., and Duncan, M. L. (Eds.). (1996). *Handbook of solution-focused brief therapy*. San Francisco: Josey-Bass.

Millman, D. (1992). *No ordinary moments: A peaceful warrior's guide to daily life*. Tiburon, CA: H. J. Kramer.

Moffett, S. (2004, October 25). After Japan's latest earthquake, government response improves. *The Wall Street Journal*, p. A17.

Moreno, Z. T., Blomkvist, L. D., and Rutzel, T. (2000). *Psychodrama, surplus reality and the art of healing*. Philadelphia: Routledge/Taylor and Francis.

Morita, S. (1975, December). Contradictoriness of thought. Translated by Kusama, M. *CID Fellowship, 4,* 1, 2.

Morita, S. (1974). The true nature of shinkeishitsu and its treatment. In Kora, T. (Ed.) *Morita Shoma Zenshu Vol. 2*. Tokyo: Hakuyosha.

Morita, S. (1928/1998). *Morita therapy and the true nature of anxiety-based disorders (shinkeishitsu)*. Translated by Kondo, A. and LeVine, P. Albany: State University of New York.

Morita, S. (1928/1974). *Shinkeishitsu-no hontai-to ryho* [True nature and treatment of *shinkeishitshu*]. Tokyo: Hakuyosha. Translated by F. Ishu Ishiyama for the *International Bulletin of Morita Therapy,* 2(2), 80-85 and 3(2), 98-103.

Mouw, R. J. (2004, Fall). In search of saints and poets. *Fuller Theological Seminary Focus, 12* (3), 2.

Murray, M. and Pizzorno, J. (1991). *Encyclopedia of Natural Medicine*. Rocklin, CA: Prima.

Nakamura, K. (2004, October 18). *Extended application and technical modification of Morita therapy*. Lecture presented at the Fifth International Meeting for Morita Therapy, Shanghai, China.

Nakamura, K., Kitanishi, K., Miyake, Y., Hashimoto, K., and Kubota, M. (2002). The neurotic versus delusional subtype of taijin-kyofu-sho: Their DSM diagnoses. *Psychiatry and Clinical Neurosciences*, *56*, 595-601.

Nakamura, K. (u.d). Psychosomatic medicine and Morita therapy. Unpublished manuscript.

Nakamura, K., Kitanishi, K., and Ushijima, S. (1994). A comparison of Morita Therapy and Cognitive-Behavioral Therapy for treating social phobia. *Journal of Morita Therapy*, *5*(1), 149-152.

Narazaki, M. (1970). *Studies in nature: Hokusai-Hiroshige*. Tokyo: Kodansha.

Nash, R. and Collins, R. O. (1989). *The big drops: Ten legendary rapids of the American west*. Boulder, CO: Johnson Books.

Nevin, J. A., Mandell, C., and Atak, J. R. (1983, January). The analysis of behavioral momentum. *Journal of the Experimental Analysis of Behavior*, *39*(1), 49-59.

O'Brien, E. and Benedict, L. (2001, April). *Deaths, disturbances, disasters and disorders in Chicago*. Retrieved December 10, 2006, from Chicago Public Library Web site: *http://www.chipublib. org/004chicago/disasters/iroquois_fire.html*

Ogawa, B. (1999). *Color of justice: Culturally sensitive treatment of minority crime victims* (2nd ed.). Needham Heights, MA: Allyn & Bacon.

Ogawa, B. (1998, July/August). Morita therapy: A valuable tool for crime victim counseling. *The Crime Victims Report*, *2*(3), 1, 42.

Ogawa, B. (1997). *Walking on eggshells: Practical counsel for women in or leaving a violent relationship*. Volcano, CA: Volcano Press.

Ogawa, B. (1989, Spring). Dogmatic self-containment as a structuring principle of Morita therapy. *International Bulletin of Morita Therapy*, *2*(1), 12-17.

Ogawa, B. (1972, March). The relation of atonement to epistemology. *Studia Biblica et Theologica*, *II*, 13-16.

Ohara, K. (1990, Spring). Creativity and experiential understanding in Morita therapy. *International Bulletin of Morita Therapy*, *3*(1), 61-63.

Olmstead, L. (2006, March 1). The pilgrimage of Fuji-san. *American Way*, 27-30.

Ornish, D. (2000). *Eat more, weigh less*. New York: Quill.

Ornish, D. (1999). *Love and survival*. New York: Perennial.

Osumi, M. and Miyasato, K. (2004, October 18). *Application of Sandplay technique based on the theories of Analytical Psychology in combination with Morita outpatient therapy to a patient with depression founded upon narcissistic personality disorder.* Lecture presented at the Fifth International Meeting for Morita Therapy, Shanghai, China.

Pachuta, D. M., (1989). Chinese medicine: The law of five elements. In Sheikh, A. A. and Sheikh, K. S., (Eds.), *Eastern and Western approaches to healing: Ancient wisdom and modern knowledge*, pp. 64-90. New York: John Wiley & Sons.

Palmer, T. (2006). *Rivers of America.* New York: Abrams.

Parker, K. (1998, March). Morita-do and the practice of yoga. *M.I.S.T.*, 1, 2.

Paulson, T. (1999, Fall). God is in charge of operations . . . but we are all in sales. *Fuller Focus*, 4-5.

Peck, M. S. (2002). *Abounding love: A treasury of wisdom.* Kansas City, MO: Andrews McMeel.

Phillips, M. (1998). Flipped out. *Texas Monthly.* Retrieved March 7, 2007, from *http://www.texasmonthly.com/ranch/flippedout/index. php*

Pinker, S. (2004, September 27). How to think about the mind. *Newsweek*, 78.

Porras, J., Emery, S. and Thompson, M. (2006). *Success built to last: Creating a life that matters.* Philadelphia: Wharton School of Business.

Quanrun, W. (2004, October 17). *Development of Morita therapy in China.* Lecture presented at the Fifth International Meeting for Morita Therapy, Shanghai, China.

Radner, G. (2000). *It's always something.* New York: Harper.

Ram Dass. (2001). *Still here: Embracing aging, changing, and dying.* New York: Riverhead.

Redfield Jamison, K. (2004). *Exuberance: The passion for life.* New York: Knopf.

Reynolds, D. (1989). On being natural: Two Japanese approaches to healing. In Sheikh, A. A. and Sheikh, K. S. (Eds.), *Eastern and Western approaches to healing: Ancient wisdom and modern knowledge*, pp. 180-194. New York: John Wiley & Sons.

Reynolds, D. (1984). *Constructive living.* Honolulu: University of Hawaii Press.

Reynolds, D. (1980). *The quiet therapies*. Honolulu: University of Hawaii Press.

Reynolds, D. K. (1976). *Morita psychotherapy*. Berkeley, CA: University of California Press.

Reynolds, D. and Yamamoto, J. (1972). East meets West: Moritist and Freudian psychotherapies. *Science and Psychoanalysis, 21*, 187-195.

River Bureau. *Land and climate of Japan*. Retrieved September 2, 2006, from Ministry of Land, Infrastructure and Transport, Japan Web site: *http://www.mlit.go.jp/river/english/index/html*

Rubin, T. I. (1975). *Compassion and self-hate*. New York: David McKay.

Ruland, V. (1999, Summer). The moment of empathy. *University of San Francisco Magazine*, 30-31.

Ruyak, J. (1996, March/April). Food. *Yoga Journal*, 44, 46, 48, 50.

Sapolsky, R. M. (1998). *Why zebras don't get ulcers*. New York: W.H. Freeman.

Scaravelli, V. (1991). *Awakening the spine*. San Francisco: Harper.

Schwartz, B. (2004). *The paradox of choice: Why more is less*. New York: Ecco.

Seelye, J. (1977). *Prophetic waters: The river in early American life and literature*. New York: Oxford University Press.

Seidler, R. D. (2004). Multiple motor learning experiences enhance motor adaptability. *Journal of Cognitive Neuroscience, 16*, 65-73.

Sheehy, G. (2002, July 21). So much good happened here. *Parade*, pp. 4-6.

Sheikh, A. A. and Sheikh, K. S. (Eds.). (1989). *Eastern and Western approaches to healing: Ancient wisdom and modern knowledge*. New York: John Wiley & Sons.

Shellenbarger, S. (2003, March 20). Female rats are better multitaskers; with humans, the debate rages on. *The Wall Street Journal*, p. D1.

Sheraton, M. (2002, January/February). L.A. and the art of sushi. *Departures*, 88-95, 119-120.

Shuster, M. (2004, Winter). Go with confidence! *Theology, News and Notes*, pp. 21-23.

Simonite, T. (2005, August 4). Shadow hangs over research into Japan's bomb victims. *Nature, 436*(7051), 610-611.

Smullyan, R. M. (1977). *The Tao is silent*. New York: Harper & Row.

Sophocleous, M. (2004, September/October). Climate change: Why should water professionals care? *Ground Water*, 42(5), 637.

Spates, R. (2004, October 18). *Independent empirical evidence from Behavior therapy in support of Morita therapy concepts.* Lecture presented at the Fifth International Meeting for Morita Therapy, Shanghai, China.

Stevens, R. J. (1998). *Teaching in American schools.* Boston: Pearson.

Suzuki, D. T. (1991). *An introduction to Zen.* New York: Grove/ Atlantic.

Suzuki, D. T., Fromme, E., and DeMartino. R. (1963). *Zen Buddhism and Psychoanalysis.* New York: Grove.

Tanishima, I. (1973, March 3). *We will be saved if we believe in Him.* Tape of sermon delivered to the Christians In-Depth Fellowship, Oakland, CA.

Tarumi, S., Ichimiya, A., Yamada, S., Umesue, M., and Kuroki, T. (2004, December). Taijin kyofusho in university students: Patterns of fear and predispositions to the offensive variant. *Transcultural Psychiatry*, 41(4), 533-546.

Tauber, M. and Trischitta, L. (2000, August 26). Truly, madly, deeply. *People*, pp. 71-72.

Todeschini, M. (1999, Spring). Illegimate sufferers: A-bomb victims, medical science, and the government. *Daedalus*, 128(2), 67-101.

Tollifson, J. (1999, January/February). The work of this moment. *Yoga Journal*, 96, 98, 100, 102.

Tresniowski, A. and Finan, E. (2000, December 18). A real downer. *People*, pp. 71-75.

Tro, R. P. (1993, Spring/Fall). Karen Horney, Psychoanalysis and Morita therapy: A historical overview of the Zen connection. *International Bulletin of Morita Therapy*, 6(1, 2), 30-46.

United States Geological Survey. (2006). *Kilauea.* Retrieved December 10, 2006, from U.S. Department of the Interior Web site: http://hvo.wr.usgs.gov/kilauea

United States Geological Survey. (2005). *Earth's water.* Retrieved November 25, 2006, from U.S. Department of the Interior Web site: *http://ga.water.usgs.gov/edu/watercycleoceans.html*

Usa, G. (1940, May 21). *Letting the life as it is: How to overcome your neurasthenia and obsession.* Radio lecture broadcast in Shanghai, China.

Ushijima, S. (2004, October 17). *The historical perspective of Morita therapy*. Lecture presented at the Fifth International Meeting for Morita Therapy, Shanghai, China.

Vachss, A. (2002, July 4). The difference between "sick" and "evil." *Parade Magazine*, pp. 4, 5.

Van Itallie, T. B. and Hadley, L. (2000, September). Spas in Japan. *GHC Bulletin, 21*(3), 29-30.

Wagener, L. M. (2003, Fall). Imagining the truth. *Theology, News and Notes*, pp. 22-23.

Wang, Z. (2004, October 17). *Light of East: The past, present and future of Morita therapy in China*. Lecture presented at the Fifth International Meeting for Morita Therapy, Shanghai, China.

Watts, A. (1961). *Psychotherapy East and West*. New York: Random House.

Wheeler, L. R. (1999, October). Holy protest. *Theology, News and Notes*, pp. 13-15.

Weisz, J. R., Eastman, K., and McCarty, C. A. (1996). Primary and secondary control in East Asia: Comments on Oerter et al. (1996). *Culture and Psychology, 2,* 63-76.

Wiesel, E. (1996). *All rivers run to the sea: Memoirs*. New York: Schocken Books.

Williams, J. (1997). *The weather book*. New York: Vintage Books.

Xinli, J. (2004, October 18). *Some viewpoints about Morita therapy for treatment of obsessive-compulsive disorder (OCD)*. Lecture presented at the Fifth International Meeting for Morita Therapy, Shanghai, China.

Yamaoka, H. (1976). *Meditation gut enlightenment: The way of hara*. South San Francisco: Heian International.

Yang, J. L. and Useem, J. (2006, October 30). Cross-train your brain. *Fortune*, pp. 135-136.

Zhang, B. and Cui, Y. (2004, October 18). *Practice of Morita therapy in integrated therapy of obsessive-compulsive disorder*. Lecture presented at the Fifth International Meeting for Morita Therapy, Shanghai, China.

Index

CPSIA information can be obtained at www.ICGtesting.com
Printed in the USA
LVOW11s1747160516

488470LV00001BA/256/P